Contents

I

II

Authentic Writing

Authentic Writing

a memoir on creating memoir

Fred Poole

Tinker Street Press ∞ Woodstock, New York

Tinker Street Press
108 Tinker Street
Woodstock, NY 12498

AuthenticWriting.com

Library of Congress Control Number: 2008904114

ISBN 978-0-6152-0492-5

Text set in Adobe Garamond

Book design by Elizabeth Panzer

Cover design by Elizabeth Panzer

Cover photo: A very early 20TH Century photo from a Poole
family house in the White Mountains of New Hampshire

Author photo by Trish Lease Photo

Printed in the United States of America

First Edition

for Marta

Writers write what they know,
but they don't know what they know
until they write it.

– W.H. Auden

I

without writing

To not write it, nor paint it, nor sing it, is to sit on it, sit on it. Is to let it hang there, hang there, hang there. Is to let it block out life.

To not write it, I am left looking out through bars in a Spanish jail which I know is Spanish because the ornately uniformed keeper wears the tri-corner hat of Franco's Guardia Civil.

To not write it, I am left a thousand miles up the Kapuas River in Borneo with a party including an Ambonese spy, and a Javanese with a Tommy gun who shoots chickens for fun, and a wiry flunky who rolls our cigarettes, and an aging preppy CIA guy, all of us surrounded some nights by Dyack headhunters and on one night by grim men in white robes who climb into the stilt house at 3 a.m., wake us on the bamboo floor, turn lantern light on a shining sacred kris they seem to worship.

Without writing, I am left forever behind an open air dance place in a Haitian brothel shack where they put me and one of the girls to lie safely while out under colored lights on the dance floor armed men in Hawaiian shirts spot a student leader, beat him, carry him away.

I am left on a dark street in Kuala Lumpur, when a race war is on, knowing there can be snipers at any of the unlit windows and wondering why I put myself here.

Without writing or painting or singing, I am forever on the floor of Murdock's Park Avenue apartment where sixth grade classmates cheer as the rich bully I have challenged pins me, pummels me.

Without writing, I am forever seen as the dumb, slow little trouble-making, drifting twin, the bad twin who was so unlike his good-twin brother Peter.

Without writing, I can so easily slip through time and land again on the floor at Murdock's. And here again – as I am down and pinned and this rich young bully is still hitting me and they are still jeering and cheering – I am slipping back still further through other scenes of terror, all the way back to the scene of my first memory on an old steam-driven train headed to the White Mountains of New Hampshire, scene of my family's defining stories, but now in a Pullman drawing room that smells of whisky with Mother in despair, Grandmother Clark making shouts and gurgles, Peter screaming, as I try to call for help but know in my bones that it is over and no help will come – something I will know again and again and never escape until I write about it. There was a button on the metal wall beside the bunk. I still see that button, for it might be what will summon help. It might save me. But I cannot press it.

I did not know that one of the smells in the drawing room was whisky, not until years later it wafted through me again as I wrote. I did not know that another smell was human blood until a man on the ground floor of my West 25th Street building was slashed up and down and crosswise. And that connection, too, was not real until I wrote.

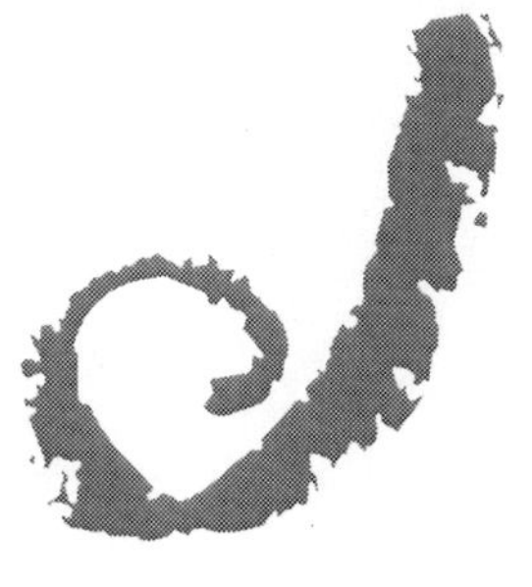

deeper

I was still in Southeast Asia when I started what had the feel of a publishable novel. The book, which came out two years later under the title *Where Dragons Dwell*, drew heavily, almost to the point of being memoir, on what had recently been part of my life in Bangkok, including a recently finished love affair with a Thai girl who, among other things, sang in night clubs. And it had as a central figure a daring and lovely young American woman I might never see again, a true sixties figure, who had arrived in town in the dangerous company of a CIA man who was pretending to be a car salesman. This was the Bangkok of the Vietnam era when it was a camp followers' boomtown overrun with spies and con men of all nations, chasing and sometimes killing each other, and American soldiers on "rest and recuperation" from the war, in town for drugs and drink and night world girls – a wildly colorful, sex-mad, anything-goes tropical river city of bright palaces and temples right on the fringe of the American wars in Vietnam, Laos and Cambodia.

In addition to my adventures in Bangkok, I was moving around other often dangerous parts of Southeast Asia as I wrote. My book was taking shape and I was feeling confident one night when I was having dinner with old American friends with whom I was staying in a well guarded, walled-off compound in Manila. Steve, an amusing and brilliant writer whom I had known in New York, and his wife Berta, who had long sandy hair, had worked with puppets, had roomed in college with my old artist girlfriend Vannie and was interested in everything. It seemed to me Steve was in a situation I had been in myself at various times, employed beneath himself for the sake of what he could learn and see well beyond the job. He was now editor of a publication called *Free World*, a slick U.S. government, Manila-based propaganda magazine that looked like a shrunken *Life* and went to anyone who wanted it in the nations of America's Cold War Southeast Asia allies, some of which, like Burma and Indonesia, were under martial law, some of which, like Thailand and Cambodia, were military-backed monarchies, and some of which, like our puppet state South Vietnam, were already out and out military dictatorships, or, like the Philippines, were headed that way. *Free World* permitted Steve and Berta to live like rich people, and be generous to friends like me whose careers were more checkered. They hosted me in the Philippines, which was fast becoming yet another well armed dictatorship – meaning there was hardly any place for political freedom in Southeast Asia except in *Free World* magazine.

Steve and Berta were living rich in Manila because they were being paid by the State Department at a time when the dollar was hugely overvalued, and also they had been given – as a perk for the supposed hardship of living outside America – this big solid house fully staffed with servants.

I was surprised at what I heard myself saying here at their round mahogany dinner table, servant girls padding around us. I was not talking now about my recent life in Bangkok, where I had thought of myself as both a pillar and the Boswell of its night world. I suddenly was talking instead about a time during World War II when I was nine and my parents had separated (though it was never called that). I talked about how we had all left Connecticut, my father for the city, my mother, my Southern Grandmother Clark and my twin brother Peter and myself to stay for some undefined period of time at a hotel in Vero Beach, Florida that was built around a tile patio with old pieces of eight embedded in it, a place that appeared to be made of found driftwood and was called "The Driftwood," a place where everyone was drinking on shaky porches and balconies all the time.

Back there in Florida, I told Steve and Berta, my mother and her mother had quickly lost track of us. For no apparent reason they failed to put us in school. They brought along fourth grade textbooks but forgot to make us use them. Peter did find the textbooks and spent his days studying alone at the hotel, where he was often the only sober living human. Me, I wandered.

I had a small bicycle I rented out to World War II soldiers billeted at a much bigger nearby beach hotel, a white stucco box building across from a beachside bar called Max's Tavern, where Mother and Grandmother Clark sometimes took us for hamburgers. It was a dark place, smelling of onions and stale beer, with a juke box always playing – "Stars at Night," clap, clap, "Are big and bright," clap, clap, "Deep in the heart of Texas," along with "Praise the lord and pass the ammunition, For we're on a mighty mission…," and also crooner songs by Bing Crosby and a very young "Frankie" Sinatra. Soldiers drank and danced with tanned women who had long, bouncy hair and bright lipstick and sometimes wore only bright colored halters with their shorts or skirts. Along one wall hidden by a screen was one of the best things I had ever seen – a row of slot machines. Even better than best, since Mother said this was illegal. "One-armed bandits," said Grandmother Clark, a gambler herself, as she downed a Manhattan cocktail.

Each day after this discovery I went to the back door of Max's with coins I had collected from the soldiers who used my bicycle – along with more coins I got by jiggling the receivers of pay phones I passed (the phone system so badly run in wartime that this was income I could count on). They let me in by the back in daytime so that I could play the slot machines.

Meanwhile, in my wanderings I made friends with a boy dressed in rags who lived in a shack in the orange groves, and sometimes we staged battles with rotten fruit. But mostly I wandered alone.

I told Steve and Berta how one day I came out of a dark palm jungle where I'd seen many reptiles and a wild boar, and often had fearful thoughts of death. And as I emerged on the main road, tanned and freckled, my hair bleached nearly white by the sun and hanging nearly to my shoulders – for, like school, barbers had been forgotten – a convertible stopped and people in bright clothes with cameras got out and took my picture. I was quite sure they thought I was a swamp rat, a colorful, backwoods, forgotten child who lived here alone in the jungle.

As my story wound down, Berta, my hostess in Manila, said, "Fred, this is what you should be writing about."

But I was not swayed from my view that my recent anything-goes time in Bangkok would have far greater appeal than anything in my childhood – as would the subjects of planned future books using, as background, my time underground in Portuguese Angola during Holden Roberto's guerrilla war, or in Borneo or Laos, or my time in Syria or Cyprus, or Haiti or Cuba or Turkey or Slovenia or Greece, or again my time in Bangkok, or right here in Manila outside this heavily guarded Manila compound, where after dinner I would go out beyond the walls to the cockfight arenas and wild bars and brothel-dance halls nearby, places filled with sleek smooth girls of the night.

What did Berta know about such exotic worlds? That I should write about that time in mundane Florida? It made me furious.

I was in my early thirties now, which seemed like I was well along in years, but it was another twenty years before I began to know, or dared to know, my deeper stories.

first person

Writers are constantly being told to write what they know, but they are often steered away from what they know best, the writer's own self. In some very deep sense all art is about the artist – and this is most obvious in all writing that rises to the level of art, whether or not it is actually written in the first person. All art that goes beyond the surface is essentially first-person art.

Right now, 40 years and a lifetime since that dinner in Manila, my wife and partner, Marta Szabo, and I and eleven other writers are sitting around a fire in a spacious room full of color and light with wide windows that bring in the garden from one side, the mountains from the far end, and from another side tall, thick pines that cut off from view the pleasant farmhouse outbuildings of a funeral home that everyone knows who lives in our Catskills town, Woodstock, NY. In this group Marta and I write along with the workshop members as we do in the various weekday and weekend groups we hold here in the Catskills and in New York City, and at times at a range of retreat centers, colleges and resorts here and abroad. On this night Marta has opened the session, and the topic that has come to mind right away is "Helter-skelter."

It came out of people's verbal introductions in this first session of a five-part weekly series. We begin each series with each person offering short spoken reflections about their writing – here at the start but nowhere else, for stories told out loud in conversation are virtually impossible to tell without knowing exactly where they are going. Written stories, however, whatever the order of things may be in the writer's head, will never go according to a set plan, will always contain surprises, when they make the transition from the head, where logic can seem real, to paper, where logic alone never suffices – never, that is, if stories are real, if the author – like a really good painter or composer or dancer – lets the material take its own mysterious directions.

For unless writing becomes some sort of precious academic exercise, honoring approved rhetorical modes and rigidly followed outlines, it will always contain surprises. No one is surprised that material comes in from mysterious places when someone is painting on canvas or composing music or working out a dance. And in the same way matters of mystery and spirit lie behind fine writing – as opposed to the predictable orderly writing that feels safe and causes no surprises at all – writing that relies on the head only and rejects the heart.

"Helter-skelter." I had no idea I had anything to write until I started to write, and hit on a crucial story I had not written and did not know was still inside me – that first memory, from before I was two, when I am sitting on the edge of an upper bunk in a Pullman drawing room on a train taking me into the White Mountains of New Hampshire and the heart of the family into which I had been born. Something horrible is happening in the drawing room. And now I am realizing as I write what I knew at the time, and why when many years later I was near a murder scene in New York City I knew what I was smelling when I smelled fresh blood.

deleting childhood

Fifteen years after that horrific time in the old steam railway drawing room, I was thinking I was on the other side of childhood. I was at a basically silly, booze-soaked college that was a sort of Gothic Disneyland – replicas of 700-year-old Oxbridge buildings set down in New Jersey beside a segregated town that had a sort of Williamsburg façade. One of the few things I took seriously in that gray college was the almost professional newspaper we had, the *Daily Princetonian.* I was the Editorial Chairman, which meant I wrote most of the editorials and was in charge of columns on the arts and politics. One day at an editorial board meeting I convinced the board in this conservative place that we should run editorials advocating two things that were almost unthinkable in the 1950s – America's recognition of China, not Taiwan, as China, and an end to Princeton's elite and racist private eating club system.

I had argued hard for not giving an inch, and my side had won, though at the start of the meeting everyone had been against me. But I beat them down like the debater I had been before college. We would run both of these editorials, it was decided. And then I heard a light remark that I took as a compliment. The head of the *Princetonian,* Dick

Kluger, who as an adult would become a much honored author, said, "It must be remembered that Fred never had a childhood."

Of course they were making fun of me because I was being so earnest, and of course I could take the joke. I knew I really had had a childhood. But somehow it seemed just as well that neither the world, nor myself, ever face the details. It was my means of self-defense.

lying letters

I found writing useful when I felt compelled to lie, which may be partly why I came to hate writing later. I was 21 and having a great time in Indianapolis, a city in which past and present came together. From another era, the city still had an old-time burlesque house, one of the last, with foul-mouthed comics in baggy trousers and ripe and overripe girls and women with tassels pasted on their nipples that whirled in great circles as they twirled their breasts. Near the burlesque house there was still a stale-beer prizefight bar inhabited by men with misshapen noses even though there was hardly ever prize fighting in this city anymore. And around a few corners a bar called the Monkey Pod that seemed built of Formica and featured Hawaiian steel guitars where overweight secretaries tried the hula as if in some 1930s cinema dream. And just a few blocks north from downtown, there were road houses filled with women drinking at piano bars, piano bars supposedly invented right here in Indianapolis because of an old law that said you could not serve drinks at a bar, but it was okay to do it at a piano. Even the most trivial things – so real here in the real world – so fascinated me. And around every corner there was a whorehouse of some kind, overflowing with girls who traveled in for the biannual session of the 3-to-1 Republican legislature, and sometimes fake brothels too, as in the storefronts where gypsy girls, their gowns falling off their shoulders, offered everything but delivered nothing except fortune telling. And I dated a very straight-forward, pretty and bright girl whose father had the Muzak concession for Indianapolis, and I was writing a novel that had started out about a sweet, half-French, pony-tailed girl who had played golf with me in Connecticut, and I had then gone way off track with made-up scenes of an escape from Cold War Poland where I had never been, and here in the present this real Indiana girl's house had a tape on a huge horizontal wheel that was constantly turning in the basement. And anywhere in Indianapolis there might intriguing danger, for adding to life's interest was that most of the political figures I dealt with in my job covering politics for United Press – these malevolent McCarthyite right-wingers – were people who had to have been members of the Klan when less than 20 years ago it ran the state and you could not get started in politics without it.

When I walked out of my brick rooming house each morning I was filled with a feeling of exaltation. I appreciated the Toddle House hamburger place next door, quick breakfasts served by a woman who had a concentration camp tattoo on her wrinkled inner arm. How strange. I would then pass the Nuremberg-like American Legion's three-block black marble headquarters, which had its own unknown dead soldier and black eagles on black marble pillars. Even stranger. But also I would pass near the city's art museum, tiny but with a Cézanne of red tile roof houses jumbled on a bright hillside. And then I would come upon a row of pretty, straight-backed girls waiting for a "Do Not Cross" sign to change even though there was no traffic at this hour. Then down past the old Claypool Hotel where politicians filled even the sidewalk in front with cigar smoke, and then a grand old railway station that had stained glass windows, near where animals cried out from the Indiana stockyards – and I would walk on down past a store front with a gypsy girl beckoning and on through one of the city's three skid rows to the *Indianapolis Times*, where United Press had its office. I was living a life.

Here I was at last free of school and college and anything else, it seemed, that was out to stop me. I might wake up mysteriously angry but then I would realize that this was freedom. Stepping out of the rooming house into the flat air of that flat city, I was no less concerned with New York and Paris and literature and art and liberal-left politics than I had ever been, but I was coming into my own now, it felt, I was free now. And I was meeting all sorts of people I wanted to meet, as in the new Beat scene up in Chicago, where I would go some weekends to hear jazz and subversive satire in places where everyone dressed in black, and also many more people here in Indianapolis where I now knew members of the old left, UE labor organizers, real Communists who were not at all like the one safe Communist professor at my college.

But these were not things I talked about in my letters that went East – letters in which I never spoke of my exaltation or fascination but rather spoke of the lack of sophistication here in the mundane Midwest, letters in which I made fun of a place whose people proudly called themselves Hoosiers.

And a few years later I was back from crossing Africa overland in a part it was said you could not cross – known later because much of the trip was through Darfur and Chad, which were not known then, it seemed, to anyone except me. I was back in Athens from Africa and struggling with dysentery, and I wrote in letters of how triumphant I felt, how I knew when I got to West Africa alive overland from East and Central Africa, knew that now I could do anything, and that this, this, was the high point of my life so far, while in fact I felt so down and out and lost that I was the opposite of what I put into those lying letters.

Which was a little like when I came to what seemed almost like a dead end in an old, dusty and airy Chinese hotel halfway between Djakarta and Punchak Pass, alone most of the time, except for when Soviet block agents stopped by to see what I was up to – and I had no answers since I could not explain even to myself why I was here, here as if paralyzed just after strange adventures that should have gotten me killed when I went all the way up the Kapuas River through headhunter territory into the heart of Borneo where like everyone I was drinking bitter rice wine in all waking hours – the sort of feat for which I had been searching, and now I wondered what I had been doing, how I got here, why it felt so hopeless. And I had shattering memories still of the end of a love affair in Bangkok. But this is not what I wrote in letters late at night in the empty old hotel between Djakarta and Punchak Pass – fortified with local beer that Javanese houseboys brought me, the houseboys being old men in robes and Sukarno-style nationalist overseas caps – in this hotel that was owned by a Chinese man who had recently and mysteriously survived a massacre of so many of the Chinese in Bali and this part of Java – and I put into letters again that this was a time of triumph – which it almost was, though not in the way I told it, for aside from the deadly aloneness, and aside from the adventures with night girls and drugs down in the ravaged cityscape of Djakarta – despite that part it was also a time when it did at certain moments feel like I was getting back on track, and I was starting to write my wild and sad Bangkok novel while in the hills of Java, writing it and getting it nearly right – back on track maybe, appearances to the contrary maybe, but that was too complicated for letters.

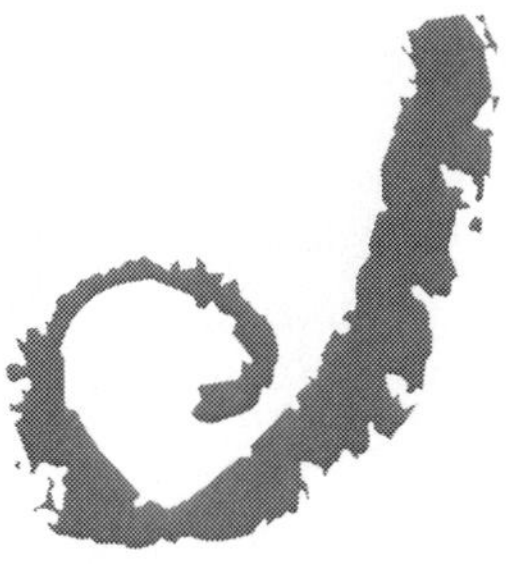

joe

When I was 14 I was really trapped. Now I was not just in school from 9 to 3 and it was not the Connecticut public school, which had been an easy place from which to play hooky. Now I was exiled to brick buildings in the New Hampshire lake country in this very different and very regimented place and I was here 24 hours a day, with someone always watching me or trying to watch me. I might get off the school grounds for as much as a few hours, but I always had to come back. And there were clouds over the future. It would be years before I was released, and by then it might be too late.

I knew there were other bigger and better worlds somewhere. They were certainly there in movies and books. I suspected there was something truly fine about the mysterious places from which came the pretty girls who very occasionally visited at our school. I thought there was something out there as big and fine as what I found in books – but if I found it and wrote about it, would anyone ever listen to me? The family said my brother Peter would be the writer. The best they said about me was that I was good at repairing simple mechanisms in the old toilets in our Connecticut house.

And they hated me, had contempt for me, in this school. They made fun of me – the slowest dumbest boy in the school. They gave me the school's worst nickname, "Speedy," and compared me to the up-till-now worst of all the boys, a guy who had graduated before I came whose horrific nickname was "Shaky." Speedy and Shaky.

The school nurse, a tight, wrinkled woman with what might have been a wise look, Mrs. Krebs, made it still worse for me when she said, "You shouldn't feel bad because your brother's smarter than you. It's all right. Some people are just a little slow. Nothing wrong with that." This seemed about right to me, these words of Mrs. Krebs, an accurate reflection not of who I was but of how I might always be perceived. Everyone said I was slow. And I was failing all my courses except English.

But bad as my life got, almost anything new would bring a surge of hope – as in the hymns sung loudly by the whole school, in assembly before the first classes of the day started and again after dinner at prayers in Livermore Hall.

"Once to every man and nation, comes a moment to decide…."

Then there were the occasional evenings when the whole school would form into an audience in Livermore to watch two seniors demolish another two-person debating team from some rival, and always much bigger, school. I was amazed that something besides sports could be received so enthusiastically.

One morning in the dining hall at the end of breakfast, Mr. Abbey, who taught English, was lingering over coffee and had a cigarette going. He was in charge of the table to which I'd been assigned and was now clearing. He asked me to sit down. He said he had something he had to say.

He was the master – we had "masters" here, not mere "teachers" – whom I enjoyed, for he read poems and stories aloud in his class. He frequently laughed, and he moved with confidence. A balding man who seemed ageless to me. His actual name was T. Charles Abbey. But the boys could, and did, sometimes call him Joe – in a place where every other adult (not counting workmen) was a "mister," a place where the boys were addressed by masters not with Mr. but not with first names either. So here I was usually "Speedy" to the boys, and "Poole" to the masters. I was hardly ever "Fred."

"Fred," Joe said, "there is something I've wanted to say to you. I think that somehow you're convinced you're not smart like your brother. But you know, you are just as smart, maybe smarter."

Everything did start to change after that – and yet it wasn't just hope that I felt at the breakfast table. On reflection I felt as if the skies had opened. But at first I was furious. I did not know why yet. I was as angry as when, years later, it was suggested to me in Manila, which was the right sort of place then, that I write about the time when I was a forgotten child in Florida.

J a debater

Not long after Mr. Abbey had let me know I did not have to be seen as dumb and slow and a lesser figure than my brother, he announced in his first year English class that we were going to stage a debate. To us, this was a little like saying that inside our classroom we were going to conduct a football game, since debating was the only competition in which this little school had been able, in recent memory, to add anything to its trophy case.

Joe Abbey, who was both the debate coach and the English teacher, now announced that in only two weeks four of us would actually be in this actual debate. It was only a debate in English class, but it would be judged just as if it were one of those big-time debates in which our varsity debaters took on and beat rival debaters and brought the sort of glory to our school that its sports teams could not manage.

I was teamed up with a kid called Fishbone, so named because he once swallowed a fishbone and it stuck in his throat and he did not tell anyone until weeks had passed and he was hardly eating and losing weight fast. Fishbone read a lot, but like me was so behind in his classes that he had to go to evening Study Hall instead of being allowed to study in his room. Fishbone and Speedy were teamed up against two boys who had the best grades in the class. One of them was my assigned roommate Peter Churchill, on his way already as a future president of the school – the dark, popular if not happy, son of a big time Boston heart surgeon. The other was my smart twin, Peter Poole, who was shorter than me but stronger and always looked people in the eye and made funny jokes and always walked with the stride of someone who knows where he is going.

The subject of the debate was federal world government. The time was less than five years after World War II and there were many people saying the world should now be organized in a different way. Fishbone and I were to speak in favor of world government. Peter and Peter against Fishbone and Speedy.

Everyone except the teacher, Mr. Abbey, laughed when I got up to speak. Someone in the back said the word "Speedy," and someone else said "Study Hall versus Room Study."

But we won quite easily.

And two months after winning the debate I was at the top of the class, not the bottom, and going to Saturday events at high schools in other towns where debaters at all levels took part in practice debates with other schools. At this time I asked to retake my IQ test and jumped ahead 40 points. Suddenly I was on Room Study. I could spend my evenings doing what I wanted so long as I stayed indoors, which I did not always do. I quit Latin and scored high enough in other subjects to rival my twin brother.

But I was still called Speedy that year, and the next year, fourth form year, it got worse. This was when the organized torture went on each night, and my roommate moved out so as not to be tarred by my unpopularity. But I kept going to these practice debate events. Mr. Abbey would not, I knew, have included me on those Saturday trips if he did not think I had potential.

I was not winning much. I was shy. Judges said they had trouble hearing me. And yet I was doing it, and Joe Abbey had faith. And I could hardly remember ever not having been on Room Study.

I was becoming a young master of linear thinking.

reading

In those school years I never for a moment thought that when I read Wolfe and Farrell and Hemingway and Fitzgerald and Steinbeck and Faulkner that I was reading fiction. And I found out when I began reading literary biographies that I was right.

Just as I knew and had it confirmed later that the places I was reading about for English were actual places – Thomas Grey's country graveyard and Wordsworth's Tintern Abbey. Keats' Grecian urn was an actual vase seen by an actual person, the first-person narrator of the poem. As real as the sometimes harsh, sometimes gentle, New England hills I could see through the old schoolroom windows.

I knew things that are easily forgotten if you fall for the idea that fiction is superior to actuality.

Joe Abbey, the English teacher who made all the difference for me, read to us from Keats and Wordsworth and Grey. He brought us Robert Browning's awful duke describing how he'd worked over his beautiful young duchess who then died. I knew that whether this was fact or fiction it was at worst a disguised version of what Browning knew from his own life, for the people in the poem were so true to actual life. There was no prettied up ending here. I loved the young duchess in my mind, where I also saw lovers stopped on Keats' Grecian urn, stopped there before life went on, before they could touch each other, before anyone could ruin it for them.

Thomas Grey vanishing in the past, "Full many a flower is born to blush unseen,/And waste its sweetness on the desert air...." An old (in his late twenties) Wordsworth above Tintern Abbey thinking of the optimistic young Wordsworth, "...when first/I came among these hills;/ When like a roe/I bounded o'er the mountains, by the sides/Of the deep rivers, and the lonely streams,/Wherever nature led: more like a man/Flying from something that he dreads, than one/Who sought the thing he loved." And Keats telling the young man he sees on the urn, "Bold Lover, never, never canst thou kiss,/ Though winning near the goal – yet do not grieve;/She cannot fade, though thou hadst not thy bliss,/Forever wilt thou love, and she be fair!"

I found it so easy to make connections when reading these versions of reality. I found I loved nature, and longed for girls, and had learned that hope was illusory, and I knew people who were much like the people in the poems. And I made connections when Joe Abbey introduced us to Dickens and talked of how Dickens wrote so convincingly about being spurned in love because Dickens himself had been spurned in love.

He had us read Galsworthy, *The Forsyte Saga*, which depicted men and women who seemed to me completely true to life as I knew it in the summers, though they were upper middle class English, not supposedly upper class American. Through Galsworthy I could see my grandmother Nana in sun hat and white dress coming in from her sunlit gardens at White Pines with her arms full of long-stemmed flowers she had just cut – Nana handing these over to a servant in one of the three pantries at White Pines, this pantry apparently there solely so that a servant could receive, and arrange, flowers.

Our third form – this being an Anglified school that called what we were in "third form" rather than ninth grade or freshman year – our third form English class went into the nearby old river town of Plymouth to see the new movie of *Hamlet*, the Lawrence Olivier version in which these people from Shakespeare seemed like real people, speaking their lines as if in actual conversation and conflict. Again, as a few weeks earlier when I had read *Julius Caesar* before it was assigned, it seemed that Shakespeare knew as much about actual challenges in actual life as Dickens or the modern Americans. Hamlet confused as to action, and angry. These Shakespeare characters were so real that I was in love with Jean Simmons' Ophelia, and felt I knew everything there was to know about loss and longing and craziness when she turned insane, sang a sweet nonsense song, and then drifted down a stream to her death, with flowers floating beside her.

I knew Joe Abbey loved what he read to us. He loved the words and the rhythms and the life and lives and places that were evoked. This was clear. And he hated what he considered got in the way of this true art that was in the literature he presented. He treated with contempt poetry and prose that had nothing concrete in it, as in the popular Joyce Kilmer drivel: "I think that I shall never see a poem as lovely as a tree…."

It was drivel to Joe if there were no actual tree anywhere to be found in sentimental talk about trees.

He spoke of the then popular, corny poet Edgar Guest, of whom, he said, Dorothy Parker wrote "I'd rather flunk my Wasserman test/ Than read the poems of Eddie Guest." It was, he said, a reference to the feared test for the deadly venereal disease of syphilis, Guest was that bad.

But even though Joe shared Dorothy Parker's view of Edgar Guest, he had found once when reading Guest aloud as an example of trite and false poetry that tears began to come to his eyes, the power of fake emotions is that strong.

And I saw a connection here with what I knew by instinct was wrong with most patriotic sentiments, and with calls for school spirit, and with faking love where there is no love.

Kilmer and Guest got reactions, Joe said, because they were good at calling up stock responses. Like the sentimental lines in Hallmark cards. Responses to writing in which there is no real sentiment because there is nothing real that is being dealt with. Just raw maudlin tears that have no real object. Like weeping over soap operas that have a lot going on in them but no people who are real, and no serious connection with anything in the life of the listener even though the listener is crying.

What this is – emotion based on stock responses rather than anything real – has nothing to do with sentiment, he said. It is sentimentality, which is something completely different.

And with Joe's help I was leaping over the trite and the false and reveling in the real writing I was discovering, the writing that went to the heart and avoided easy outs, the writing that first made me realize I was not alone in the world, and then made me want to be a writer – whatever else the family planned for me. And I could not possibly have had all this if I had been reading writers who, like so many current novelists, followed the dictates of play-it-safe writing teachers and ended all stories with neat resolutions.

the new sentimentality

Many years later, at a time in life when the proper people had long since settled down, I was with my new girlfriend Danielle. At least I thought Danielle was my girlfriend. The right girlfriend, it was beginning to seem. Not only talented and imaginative herself but convinced I was talented and imaginative too. And she was so pretty and funny. Also brilliant. Life and relationship the way life and relationship should be. We had so much in common – our art work, and for a time the bond of unearned money.

She was so attractive that when I first saw her I heard members of my family, some long dead, making fun of her for being too smart and stylish and pretty.

But I had just started the Authentic Writing Workshops, and Danielle had already told me I was doing it all wrong. I was allowing, if not instigating, stories that had no resolution and went into dark territory. She said I should revert to timed exercises, one of which should be to ask workshop participants to describe a bird in flight. Not, she said, that she thought hard stories should be censored. The shadow side is real. And I knew enough about her late alcoholic and invasive minor-celebrity mother and horrific childhood to know she had plenty of raw material for very dark work. And yet she had all these ideas to help me help people avoid dealing with darkness.

One of them was this "bird in flight" thing so familiar to people in very orthodox writing workshops who are given a "prompt," which seems to me to carry the implication that this is being done by a prompter, a person whose job is to make sure that actors follow their lines. (Whereas in our workshops Marta or I will throw out a few words that might cause a scene to appear and thus might touch off something to write about, but, we emphasize, should be disregarded if a scene that seems way off the subject swims into consciousness.)

Do exercises, Danielle said – and she may have used that awful term "free writing" that in correct and constipated writing workshops is used to subtly put down writing that flows beyond the confines of careful, safe outlines. Important as a warm-up exercise, Danielle said, but then to be thrown away.

Danielle wasn't always criticizing my workshops. Although her own writing tended towards careful poetry, she talked a lot about her really horrible childhood. But she talked sometimes not so much about specific matters in her own stories but about how her stories were the foundation for something important for the world at large.

Sometimes tears would come as she talked – not when she was stepping into her life stories but rather when she was using the stories to back up conclusions. She began to cry as she said that what we were doing, finding out what really happened in the dark or misty past, was so very important because it would help assure that no child again would have to suffer what we had suffered. She was crying and she was so open and attractive. A talented, tortured, artistic woman who could not find happiness, could not stay within a community, was always moving on. And sometimes was more comfortable saying "we" instead of "I," speaking on behalf of people other than herself.

Tears did not come when she actually got into stories of her tortured childhood the way they flowed when she talked in generalities on other people's behalf. And this did not seem strange to me. When I was first going after my stories by speaking about them, though not yet in writing, I had said much the same thing before a group of people looking into the past, and I could not finish what I had to say, I was so overwhelmed with emotion. Emotion that did not last so long as a certain smugness that now I really had the story right. And the smugness had a bitter taste, for it is impossible to tame a story that is real.

This short-lived smugness that resulted from having everything in place. To my maybe girlfriend maybe the best way to handle this was to look not at real people but at archetypes. She frequently traveled far to conferences that delved into archetypes.

But what was happening – what tends to happen when a person speaks in generalities – is that actual live people tend to vanish from the story. The people in the stories, including the tellers of the stories, come across as case histories, something tucked away to be brought out to back up points that are being made.

When tears came to me as I was speaking in generalizations, it was not unlike what my brilliant and sensitive old boarding school English teacher, Joe Abbey, had told of his experience when he read aloud really awful sentimental poetry and found tears welling up in spite of himself. I can also be moved for a very brief time by a lightweight movie where everything works out and the villains are all reformed, and the hero has overcome odds against him to the point where he has a lover now who looks exactly like a movie star.

Tears in the movie theater where everything is simpler than life can ever be, tears when there are archetypes but no people – so different from tears in life. The listener might be moved when hearing the generalizations, but it is not the same thing as being moved when presented with an evocation of something concrete and real.

Real stories buried in theory are, as Marta points out, like a politician standing beside a legless veteran and talking about the need to sacrifice to make the world safe for freedom, democracy and corporate growth.

For there are far more insidious things than shallow crying over shallow stories. And yet all false stories do take the life out of real stories. Without real people in the stories it is easy to manipulate the stories – as so many sociopathic political figures have learned. And then everyone can sing the equivalent of that sentimental xenophobic Irving Berlin song "God Bless America" while everyone is working towards, or silently colluding in, the most awful atrocities.

I sympathize with those who try to get into the spirit of this false and dangerous nonsense – as I tried so hard once, when younger than my years, to make things right with that beautiful, tortured, artistic woman who wanted to get her stories under control.

beyond fiction

Wiping out the uniqueness of the concrete by overwhelming it with talk of the universal. The archetype. Everyman. Making it deceptively easy by overriding reality, by dismissing what really happened.

Or likewise burying reality by snuffing out real life that gets in the way of fictional constructions about what life ought to be, as in those letters I wrote from Athens after the Africa trip. Snuffing out what is not useful to fictional stories.

One thing that helped me bury my deeper stories for many years was respect for "fiction." I was from a literary family. My grandfather, Ernest Poole, had won the first Pulitzer Prize for fiction with a novel, *His Family*, that was partly taken from his own life.

But vital parts – especially involving any sex that might be appealing – were ruled out. All of his couples slept in separate bedrooms whether married or not (which was how it was in his own family, and in the families of his children and even with all but a few of us in the generation that came next). In one scene in my grandfather's best known novel, *The Harbor*, a boy in Brooklyn sees a naked prostitute in a window, as had my grandfather himself when young in Chicago, and the result is terror mixed with prudishness, without an apparent touch of admitted lust. The boy runs home to take comfort from his mother, as did my grandfather– as recounted in an academic dissertation on his work. I tried to make sense of this scene of terror at the sight of nakedness – because it was in a published book, because it was literature and because the author was my grandfather. But it did not seem quite right. For I could feel the appeal of a naked girl in a window.

My father was a book person too. He was editor-in-chief of a publishing house where for a long time he had great success not with "fiction" but with light, personal experience "nonfiction." He specialized in personal experience stories of happy, again apparently fairly sexless, families of regular people – *Chicken Every Sunday*, *Cheaper by the Dozen*, *Excuse My Dust* – families that were not from the same planet as the very formal family from which he came and where he had been a lonely boy with a pony cart, often left alone with a governess in one of his parents' big formal houses in the otherwise scruffy White Mountains of New Hampshire while his parents traveled abroad. There was no seeming connection between my father's own life and the lives of the regular people in the books he published with such success.

Here in these books, it later seemed to me, was real respect for fiction, even though it was not labeled as such. These happy first-person family-story books were taken up by book clubs, made the bestseller lists, might become movies – and then it all came to an end with the rise of television. At that point all the happy, funny, too-good-to-be-true family stories, stories in which sex never reared its ugly head in any way that seemed real, were taken over by fifties television sitcoms that depicted the world as fearful people hoped it would be in the bland and repressive Eisenhower years. Laugh tracks overrode any questions. Soon my father was out of work.

What I first wanted to write had to do with things I read when I was alone at Holderness, my boarding school – gentle Georgian buildings, political and literary discovery and adolescent cruelty down in New Hampshire's lake country. At the beginning, shunned by the world, it seemed, I was reading everything from adventure stories to Shakespeare, everything except books assigned in classes. Each night I had to go to evening Study Hall because I was labeled one of the slow, dull students. I sat in a musty old assembly room, under the eyes of a master, in a building we called the Schoolhouse, which had once been an old-time one-room schoolhouse and now had individual classrooms added around the periphery of this central room. Here each of the 68 boys had a very old desk – initials from the deep past carved in the slanting, rutted, varnished top, which was on a hinge so that the top could be pulled up, leaving a box containing school books, and just above the hinge an indentation where a pencil or nib pen could rest without sliding down into your lap, and to the right of the indentation a cut-out circle where there was an old inkwell, every inkwell periodically checked for refilling. This was 1950 but except for the fluorescent lights it could have been 1850.

I sat on a seat attached to the desk behind me. It was a little ghostly here at night, since the vast majority of the boys were good enough students to be allowed to study in their dorm rooms with no one watching.

I read only from the first year English anthology. I was not doing homework, and I only opened my other school books so that it would look like I was studying. But I was way beyond homework, for I was discovering, on my own, first Kipling and then Shakespeare and then Wordsworth, and then Conrad, taking in their words while trying to look like I was involved with Algebra, which was taught by the football coach, and geography and world history, where our teacher was the basketball coach and the books seemed to be in baby talk, and Latin and French, which made no sense at all to me.

I had these books, and in time I was sent another book from home, my grandfather's last novel, *The Nancy Flier*, just published posthumously by my father some thirty years after the book where the naked girl in the window made a cameo appearance. By the time it arrived I was still reading from the English anthology but I was also up to my ears in modern novels, which in Study Hall I hid inside the textbooks.

The Nancy Flier was an historical novel about a boy who worked on stage coaches in the White Mountains. It was set in a stage coach inn between Lisbon and Littleton, a big old wooden building that still stood, though long abandoned, and had been pointed out to me every summer of my life. In this novel there was a brief appearance by a young man from over in Portsmouth who was a cabin boy on a clipper ship. I decided I would take this minor character and make up a book-length story about him – a clipper ship companion piece to my grandfather's stage coach book.

Except that I did not believe either boy had ever existed – not like the title character in *Studs Lonnigan* who lusts after his sister, or the narrator in the Thomas Wolfe books, who wants to experience everything in the world and pretty much does it with women, including one who is older and seems to envelope him in flesh, or Hemingway, who combines war and sex, or Fitzgerald, who writes of basically unattainable but sex-driven girls high on the social scale in societies that, though touched by romance, could seem as outwardly staid as that from which I came.

It briefly occurred to me that instead of writing about my grandfather's fictional cabin boy I could write about my own life, but the thought was quickly dismissed. I couldn't do anything like that in those boarding school years – write stories from life! Who in the world would be interested in real stories by such a shy person as me whose grip on the story he wanted to live was still so tenuous?

When J.D. Salinger's *The Catcher in the Rye* came out two years later it seemed to many of us – like me at Holderness and our friend from the summer Lou Cornell at Taft – that this changed everything – a matter about which my brother the good-twin and I, so often rivals now, completely agreed. A book confirming the real place in the real world of a sensitive, smart prep school boy. Something, it seemed, no one had noticed till now. Boys at many boarding schools, like me and Lou and my brother too, were suddenly contacting each other. At last our side was winning. The dumb and cruel but popular athletes had no idea what we were talking about. And the book critics were dismissing it all as vulgarity.

In my three years now at this little school I had been feigning disinterest in the bullies to the point where I almost, but not quite, believed they would not win in the end – and now maybe *The Catcher in the Rye* would be their death knell. Holden Caulfield was reporting on much of what had been my experience – family and school worlds where he was not understood, bullying and snobbery in a small prep school, a longing for actual sex with actual girls – surrounded by boys who operated from snobbery and physical cruelty. Holden and I were not exactly alike. I had never gotten so close to sex as he did when a sad young prostitute came to his room at a sad Times Square hotel. Moreover, I was not nearly so successful as him at putting my life into my own words, not words it was supposed to be in. But we were close enough. We loved girls. We hated phoniness. We were smart, and not so well liked. What a wonderful word, phoniness. It covered so much. We were real outsiders and by now I, like Holden, was no longer ashamed of it.

Still, there was something that disturbed me about the Salinger book.

In my last year in boarding school, when I was no longer seriously unpopular, a group of us met in New York in Easter vacation. We got noisily drunk on gin & tonics and something called a Pink Lady. We moved among many of the many places that would serve people under 18, which was then the legal age – the very formal dark wood and leather men's bar at the Biltmore, the very informal Village place called Julius's which had sawdust on the floor (this so long ago Julius's was not a gay bar yet), the Dixieland places Jimmy Ryan's and Eddie Condon's, and the sophisticated-seeming bar at One Fifth Avenue. Too drunk to go to any home, we decided to get a hotel room. We decided on an excitingly grubby place, the mildewed old Carter Hotel in a lost land between the movie theaters and across from Hubert's Flea Circus on 42ND Street off Times Square. This, I was sure, was the hotel where Holden Caulfield had met that appealing and heartrending young prostitute.

She did seem appealing to me, unlike to Salinger. And this low-life hotel seemed to me a place of infinite possible adventures. Holden had turned the girl down, which seemed to me not unlike my grandfather running home to his mother when he saw a naked woman in a window, a scene he changed in fiction from his home city, Chicago, to his writer's territory, Brooklyn. It just made no sense, and I suspected it meant that even in Salinger there was a deep underlying prissiness that falsified life as life would actually be. That night when we were all drunk there were no girls for us in the hotel, though there may have been for older, more solid citizens. Still, I believed from whorehouse scenes in my reading that there was a glamour to prostitution, and I was determined that when the right girl appeared I was not going to run, and I was certainly not going to send her away.

ban on *new* stories

Set remarks always came fast in the course of the eight-hour summer trip from Connecticut's Fairfield County up to New Hampshire's White Mountains that I had made every year of my life. That trip, sometimes made in a steam-driven, single-track train, but most years made crunched up in a fold-down back seat while locked in a pre-war Plymouth convertible with Mother and Dad and Peter.

The village green and bandstand at Avon, Connecticut are pointed out with the same words always spoken while going through Avon. Too quaint and too cute, Dad says, although Dad's publishing specialty is books celebrating big happy families in worlds where quaint and cute are compliments.

And what a silly name Agawam is, Mother and Dad and Peter all say, as they always say each time we go through it – and Thetford is even sillier – and how ridiculous, that concrete dinosaur outside Holyoke – and there's something really stupid about a mosque dome on an office building in Hartford.

Dinner always at a stuffy, dark, low-ceiling inn in Northampton – acidy tomato juice – called "toe-*mah*-toe juice" – mushy, bitter vegetables, tough lamb chops wearing paper socks, Mother and Dad eating raw oysters that look like gobs of snot as they argue over whether this is one of the months oysters can kill you.

Then on, and many places not to stop – miniature golf, animal and reptile places, the place of 10,000 baskets. Mother and Dad call these places "tourist gags," though Mother also complains that Dad will never stop for the basket place. And how about that sign for Old Sturbridge Village? How silly recreating an old New England village here in New England where nothing has ever changed.

These are not things someone says once or twice that could be remembered as being said on a certain specific occasion. These remarks are like stories repeated over and over but always as if they're being told for the first time.

When these set remarks are brought to speech there is no time context – it is always the same time.

As we ride along, my parents – who shy away from glamour – are constantly pointing out homely girls. Vermont, and New Hampshire too, they say – meaning the people who live there always, not we summer people – Vermont and New Hampshire breed homely girls, they say – homely girls in homely towns.

Look how homely that girl is, as we go through Bellows Falls (what a silly name) – look at that homely girl standing at the rail on the Brattleboro bridge –

But there – I see from the cramped back seat – there is a very pretty girl we're passing this time in Bellows Falls. She's in shorts, not Bermuda shorts, just shorts, tight, very short, and I know without knowing how I know that this girl who arouses me is a girl who lives here in this year-round town all the time – lives in the midst of these things of beauty we pass through, these sweeping fields, these cows, these signs that say "Fresh Corn 4 sale", these old gray silos and old spotted cows and tractors and horse-drawn wagons.

Just before the covered bridge town of Bath a permanent sign warns "Bump." How New England, they say. Not change things by smoothing out Route 10 – just put up a "Bump" sign.

Oh these year-round people, they say.

And they still see homely girls. But when we stop for gas at Bath (stop because the tank's only half full and you can't be too careful) I peer out from our car's tiny back seat, and there is another startling girl my age. She is on the porch of a small store behind the hand-cranked gas pumps. And she's in a bright yellow two-piece bathing suit, bright yellow holding actual breasts, and she's very tan and she's licking an ice cream cone!

Then through a town with a lumber mill, called, laughably, Lisbon – then past the Sugar Hill railway station (how quaint they say, that pretentious old station master putting out flower boxes, as he always does).

We continue up and through the little village of Sugar Hill with its picket fences, general store/post office and wooden sidewalk – just like it always was, everyone says – and another turn at St. Matthew's, the simple, understated little wooden Episcopalian summer church where Mother and Dad were married and where the boss is our paternal grandmother whom we call Nana (but not the way other children call grandmothers Nana, for ours is a grande dame who is always in charge wherever she might be – which is often in major cities of the world and among important people).

After passing Nana's church, we are going down a dirt road through deep, dark woods that include white birches –

No houses in sight. The house of my grandfather's old Princeton roommate, Otto Mallery, is there, but so deep in the woods we cannot see it. No houses till our caretaker's cottage and barn and our own big summer houses, all of which have names.

Up high, there is our dark, round, turreted House on the Hill. Then, below the hill and right on the dirt road, our very old 20-room Farm House. Then, set back, our long, rambling summer "cottage," White Wings –

Finally a turn down across from the Farm House to White Pines, the newest and biggest big house, built with stone on an iron-boulder bluff Nana and Gaga own, looking out over blueberry and thorn fields to woods they own – stretching all the way to the high peaks of the

Franconia Range that they might as well own –

White Pines, reached by this mile-long twisting driveway through pine woods, planted by Nana and Gaga when they built this latest house but so tall I cannot believe these woods have not been here forever. Going through them now on this long driveway that is too narrow at all points for cars to pass.

Mother says something sarcastic about what she calls "Dad's humble origins." It seems to make her mad that this place is so rich and complete.

Dad leans on the horn. He is angrier than Mother. Much of his growing up took place here. He leans on the horn again.

Dad's angry, though anyone going down this driveway leans on the horn – blows the horn in case someone who does not appreciate the danger tries to come the other way. But it seems like no one, at least no one who thinks other than we do, ever will. For this driveway leads to a house in which no change is allowed. A protected place. A place of stories that never change – of when Gaga went missing in the Russian revolution, or their gondola rounded a corner and met a Venetian barge piled high with the brightest oranges in the world, or my grandmother, while tramping (the correct word for hiking) in pre-World War I Bavaria, decided to be one of the first women to smoke cigarettes. Gaga covering World War I from both the German and the American sides, or Gaga, out at dawn in a Chicago park, seeing a descendent of Lincoln's assassin bow to a Lincoln statue, or Gaga in his Socialist days living in settlement houses, or Nana, who did not drive yet, in a car with a mailman who suddenly has a heart attack and she knows she must stay with the dead man for she sees in the sky the words "The U.S. mail must be protected."

I could not look at the fireplace at White Pines without remembered accounts of that long ago night, long before I was born, before airplanes and swimming pools, when a ball of lightning came down the chimney, scooted across the living room area, went between a brocade chaise longue, two brocade sofas, past tables with tasseled lamps and drawers for cards and coasters and Chinese Checkers and Parcheesi. The ball of lightning going past the chairs with gold threads where Frances Perkins and Cornelia Otis Skinner and Herbert Hoover had sat and stood.

The lightning ball had gone past Nana's high fold-out desk which always has Wintergreen mints in a cubbyhole – past brown Chinese screens and past a standup wood radio with a glowing orange dial and a green light that winks if the reception is not clear –

Past the trash basket where Nana had found Gaga's crumpled up Pulitzer certificate (almost thrown away, he was so modest, Nana said) .

On past the Steinway with the head of Nefertiti, the ball of lightning shooting past dim stand-up lamps, a pendulum wall clock that shows phases of the moon, more dim tasseled lamps coming out from the walls with orange bulbs shaped like flames.

Past the bay-window, mountain-view alcove where tipsy Great Uncle John, they said, had set out on an improvised mock witch hunt with his Yale friends Cole Porter and Monty Woolley, a simulated mob going all the way up to the Farm House shouting, "Burn her, burn her!"

Then the ball of lightning going on underneath the 14-foot long polished dining table, where finger bowls are always used.

Going below the long horizontal paned glass windows that perfectly frame the only permitted mountains.

All the way from the fireplace where it came down to the fireplace at the other end of the room 70 feet away, where the ball of lightning had then gone up this other chimney.

Something, like everything else that counts here – like Bavaria before the First World War, like Gaga before the writing stopped – something that would never happen again.

Never again, it sometimes seemed at White Pines, would there be new stories. In the generation that followed Gaga and Nana's, people retold to each other stories heard in White Pines more than they told their own stories of more recent times and places. And each time a story was repeated it became further reinforcement to barricades that were holding back new writing and new writers. In the old stories, the past was always a better place. The dwellings grander. The sensibilities more refined.

A new story always contains the unexpected, which can be as disturbing to families as it is to bystander literary critics and orthodox academic writing teachers. White Pines was a house and a way of life founded by a writer but not necessarily a place for anyone's writing except his own.

those *set* forms

When I was on vacation from my boozy college an alert, personable friend from home, Bruce Agnew, a guy who like me wanted to be a writer, and unlike me had been considered the smartest kid in our eighth grade class, told me he had just gotten the word from the famous author Robert Penn Warren in a seminar he had just taken at Yale. The word was that something had to change in every story. If nothing changed, you did not have a story.

This was very bad news, the way I took it, for it seemed to mean you had to follow other people's versions of reality in reporting change that did not exist. Or worse, follow entire patterns of stories as ordered up by the literary establishment. Kill off your own version – conform to what others in power, if not Warren himself, wanted for you.

Well, I had a few triumphs behind me, pre-college triumphs in the boarding school years, where I had started at the bottom of my class and wound up at the top, even sometimes passing my twin brother Peter, the good twin whom I had perhaps put under siege causing him to fight for his life to maintain his family-awarded titles of good twin, socially adept twin, smart twin.

And then there were changes during vacations, especially during the long summers up in the White Mountains of New Hampshire. I had wondered if I would ever have girlfriends like guys in novels and movies did, and sure enough I came to know heart-warming necking that made the antics of Doris Day and Jimmy Stewart look like kindergarten stuff. There were girls, but mainly there was this one girl, Kitty – too nice and too good looking to be true – this one girl who seemed to be the right girl and who seemed to return my love. And meanwhile down at the Holderness School in the New Hampshire lake country, the school's trophy case had been filling up with trophies I had won on the New England debating circuit – big plastic and wood objects each topped with a naked, stylized brass woman who held a laurel wreath high above her head. And I had just about the best grades in the school now, whereas I had started with the very worst, so bad I had had to sit with the slow boys in compulsory evening Study Hall every weekday night.

There was poetry now, that I read and also that I wrote and that went into the school paper, which was edited by my twin brother and me now, whereas so recently everyone would have laughed at the thought of me having such a position. The boys had stopped laughing at me now. A number of them were becoming my friends. I knew deep down that any success I had was only provisional. I could still, as in the past, start making missteps that would cause everyone to forget everything about me except that I was shy and slow and bad at sports. One misstep and I would again be known as "Speedy."

There had been all these changes back in boarding school, so maybe, I thought briefly, considering the Yale version of compulsory change, there might be something here for me to write about.

I wondered about it, but the answer in my head was a harsh "No!" – for this was not fit material for a story that would work. My experience at Holderness would not qualify as literature.

I had already found in my reading that there was a tradition in fine novels, usually British novels, of telling stories about the horrors of boarding schools. And I had horror stories. But our school still did not fit neatly into this literary category. For one thing, it was too small. And although there was some cruelty and bullying brutality, I was not convinced at the end that it was as horrible as such places in correct fiction. And so I did not think that these changes in my life would really count as the change needed in a story as stories are supposed to be written.

And now college, which was a famous and much bigger place – heralded by authors ranging from F. Scott Fitzgerald to my grandfather – but which in fact seemed dreary and conformist and stuffy and silly. How could I write about this college and get in the Robert Penn Warren-mandated change. For surely, some voice was telling me, change in a correct college story should be for the better.

And how could I write about the world around me if I could not put change into the story?

The world. The awful Eisenhower, who spoke only in clichés and hated all art, cheered on by so many at my college. And two years back the strutting General Macarthur had attempted treason for working to invade and drop the big bomb on China, and when relieved of his command had come home to a hero's welcome. Nothing changed. The crazed, mendacious Senator McCarthy, who was ruining lives of the sort of people I admired from a distance, was riding high, and the press and almost all politicians treated him as a serious and legitimate political figure. An earnest Jewish couple, the Rosenbergs, had gone to jail for treason because of their efforts to prevent the use of atomic weapons, and then, like in a bad movie about other times, they had been executed. The Rosenbergs were dead and so nothing in the world changed, unless you counted their deaths.

I didn't really think all stories had to have happy endings. But I had fallen for this very limiting idea that without change you did not have a story – with the rider that change meant following some triumphal notion of how things are supposed to be.

When I first went to Princeton I put my boarding school time away, not as in life but into a literary wax museum version. In the college time I tried briefly even to like spectator sports while also focusing on my own interests, stirring writing and radical politics and nightlife. I drank heavily to get around how distant what was around me was from anything that deep down I honored. As for my boarding school time, which had given me life, I dismissed it. I picked up on a college roommate's label for the place, "Holderness in the wilderness," which helped me bury the story.

Many years later when the Authentic Writing program was in full swing the academic mandates for correct stories had been refined even further. Now kids were being taught something called "rhetorical modes," which seemed like something from the 19th century, and there were classes where you were told that every story had to have two elements that in fact are but rarely found in life – an epiphany and a resolution.

By the time I heard these new dictates I was quite willing to admit that college was as bad as it seemed. And that it had seemed bad in large part because I had had something else to compare it to – which was the period in boarding school when I came into my own, and words in literature resonated with who I was and what I wanted. I had had such a big experience in boarding school that I was not ready to accept social nastiness and pretentious academic attempts to control art as my yardstick for measuring what I came to know. I was not ready to become a good, gray Princeton man. But I was not ready either to completely give up the fictional disparagement of what I loved or the fictional glorification of what I hated. And so I drank.

The boarding school story had indeed contained more change than any writing teacher could order up – but I had not seen it as the correct story since it did not fit the classic boarding school story. Much more time would go by before I was able to write from the inside, from my own true version of reality, not someone else's, or from my constructions for how it should be.

J without a family

In boarding school as well as in college and for a long time afterwards I got away with writing without crucial context. In published work as well as early unpublished work there were huge gaps in what I presented about my characters. I still took it as a compliment when at a college newspaper board meeting it was said that "Fred never had a childhood." I had tried to ignore a large part of the context of my own life, and I ignored that context in what I was writing, which meant that the writing, in crucial ways, was mere fiction.

When I was in my twenties, a perceptive agent who had tried to get my unpublished work published suggested I say something about where the main character came from. This, I decided, was ridiculous. It smacked of lightweight sentimentality and conventionality and pop psychology.

But you do not need to be a psychoanalyst to know that a person's background is crucial to who that person is. It takes massive self-deception to edit out an autobiographical character's background.

Still, I managed to do it, and I have seen this happen with other writers. The moment the background, the context, of an autobiographical character seems necessary, the writer often decides this is the time to flee into fiction and/or cold, gray, how-to-write rules. For the context to the story can be more dangerous to the writer than the story the writer plans to tell – in my case, the context taking in the stark woods of old New Hampshire, which when I wrote seemed clearly more dangerous than the wild savannah country of Central Africa.

After those unpublished novels and some professional journalism, I finally wrote a novel that would be published. I wrote it in just a few months in Singapore, Las Palmas, London, Malta, Zermatt, New York, and while revisiting the White Mountains (which did not figure in the story). I still ignored the advice that I use my experiences from childhood. Again, I let my characters spring into life as if born as adults.

My novel had three main characters – the hero, his friend, and his girlfriend, and many side characters, many of them beautiful women since the novel was set in late sixties Bangkok, in a time of wild erotic happenings and cloak and dagger things, and constant assassinations – so much going on that neither my new agent nor the editor who accepted the book for publication seemed to notice that no one in it had had a childhood. The main character was me, living by my wits. The girlfriend was Bonnie, an American who had dropped out of an Antioch College work-study program in Tokyo to work in a night club, the one who had come to Bangkok with a CIA man who now wanted me dead. Actually, my twin brother was in Bangkok then too, working for a Defense Department agency geared to helping Southeast Asian armies work over their countries' peasants. I was clearly on the other side, which made me and my brother to a considerable extent enemies – not unlike how it had been when we were children. He didn't appear in the novel, neither as child nor man, though so many of the people I knew in Bangkok had cameos.

I got away with this lack of a family of origin once, but soon afterwards – while living in a claustrophobic Middle Eastern place – I could not do it again. I had signed a contract, and taken a little advance money, to do another novel, using the same agent and with the same editor. It seemed to me a fitting sequel to the last book, but the opening chapters were sent back by the agent with an angry letter. He did not question that the writing was mine, but he just could not believe the life I was portraying. It was as if I had made a clumsy attempt to make up an implausible story. Although this was a novel, although this was fiction, it still had to be more believable than what he had seen. The portrayal of my main character – who happened to be in his mid thirties like me then, and who had done the same things I had done – was so unconvincing, he said, that the story was clearly based on nothing real.

And then the agent said he wondered why in the narration there was nothing at all about where the character had come from, nothing about his childhood, family or background. I did not think then that this was a significant question, though I did remember what Berta had said in Manila about my Florida childhood stories. Now, it seemed, the agent and editor were as off-base as Berta.

Actually, this lack of a family of origin was the only part of that novel-in-progress not based on fact. It was only later I realized that the manuscript could not possibly have rung true to the agent, for in life there can be no such gap. And maybe that was why the rest of the story seemed artificial to him too.

But where was the public, I asked myself, for anything so uninteresting as my family?

It was much later that it became clear to me that at that time I had been writing only in part because of what I felt I needed to say. An equally big part was that I had wanted to keep on having work published. I had needed to be A Writer. Strange, I had thought, that this agent, who enjoyed a great deal of success with works that were commercial and often artistic, should think I was getting it wrong.

The character in my book whom the agent said was not believable, the one who seemingly had sprung to life fully grown, had traveled to the heart of Borneo on the Kapuas River in a time of ritual cannibalism. He had been in insurrections in Angola, Haiti, Cuba, Greece and Malaysia, even though he was not a soldier and not really a war correspondent and did not work for any intelligence service. He had somehow crossed Africa alone from Khartoum to Fort Lamy, traversing a thousand-mile stretch for which maps showed small villages but no roads. Most recently, although he had a poor sense of direction, he had flown small planes for recreation in areas – Lebanon, Cyprus – where you might encounter anti-aircraft artillery if you went a half kilometer off course. At various times he had already, before coming to the Middle East phase, lived in Slovenia, Greece, Thailand, Hong Kong, Singapore and the Philippines – as well as the, to him, equally foreign Indiana and Georgia. And, after leaving a boozy, gray, socially correct college, he had gone through a rapid career in wire service journalism, then put in nominal Army time as a draftee while continuing as a newsman, and then gone on to independent adventure. And this was only the start of what had happened – jail in Mississippi in the Civil Rights time, for example, and an unexplained, even to himself, period moving between the Canary Islands and Malta.

These were matters already dealt with in the opening chapters of that autobiographical novel I was writing. But there were so many other matters that were not in it.

Without a family, the character in the book could not have a twin brother, like the author's twin brother, who was in the CIA and worse, and often in the same places the character chose to live. He could not have a first cousin, maybe it was two or even three first cousins, who, like the author's cousins, had killed themselves. Nor did he, like the author, have a cousin who was a molester, nor a cousin who was in and out of battered women's shelters and had been fucked and beaten by her brother from the age of seven until she was sixteen. He did not have a father who as a child had been left with governesses while his parents toured Europe. And he did not have a mother who had spent a crucial part of childhood in courtrooms where her father was on trial for political shenanigans. And he had not been raised being told he was slow and stupid. And, moreover, without a family there were no family drug and alcohol complications.

And my character had not spent the summers of his formative years in grandiose, quite beautiful and intensely formal mountain houses where most in these houses, isolated from other human contact, spoke with fake British accents. And he did not have a father who published light personal experience books about big happy families of regular people, nor a grandfather who wrote well-received sexless novels – writing that was so important that no others in the family, it was understood, need ever write anything themselves.

Insomnia

I toss around. I get up, have a soy cheese snack, fake cheese so I will not die with clogged arteries, and then I try again. Back in bed I look at the old clock radio whose tape player has not worked for years. When I went to bed it was midnight, and I have to be up at eight so there had been time for a full night's sleep, but now it is three, and then four, and I see daylight creeping in from behind the shades. Almost no time left, and I have a lot to do in this day ahead. Better take a pill – though it might be even better to have a cigarette.

I toss and I turn, kind of drugged up now, and it would really be much better if I could smoke. I haven't had a cigarette in over 20 years. But when I had my last one it was at the end of that day's regular three packs. So who knows when the lung cancer will strike.

That past comes in. A cigarette on the edge of the desk. All desk edges had cigarette burns. A cigarette right after making love. "Fucking" was the word even way back when it first became relevant to me, a word back then, and sometimes now, more thought and acted upon than spoken. Leaning over to some night table somewhere and finding the cigarettes. Probably putting two in my mouth at the same time so that there will be one to pass on to the girl, in the style of Humphrey

Bogart, who must have had an incredibly long list of women fucked. I am not getting any closer to sleep. Maybe I can try what I used to do for sleep when I was in an upper bunk at Ft. Benning in the silly peacetime army. I would think in chronological order of every girl I had ever fucked – which had been a very short list until the months just passed in Indianapolis at the time the Indiana Legislature was meeting. A sweet red-headed working girl named Mandy in a flea bag hotel. And then the list got longer just before I was drafted, for I spent those last weeks in Batista's Cuba. But the list is still short enough so that it needs women almost fucked, and then women I was determined to fuck one day, especially women whom I had not met yet, women in my imagination. But this is not helping at all. Could it really have put me to sleep at Ft. Benning 50 years ago? Of course I am now beside my beautiful wife whom I love and who is sleeping peacefully – not in a bunk in the barracks.

I toss and I turn. There are still so many loose ends in my life, going back into the deep past. Was I or was I not molested as a child? Does Aunt Betsy count? Three months behind on the mortgage. Isn't it time I made money from writing again? Writing is probably all over for me. And the old Volkswagen Golf, its left front tire has a not-so-slow leak, and there is a strange screeching sound that starts when I pull out of the driveway and does not stop for five minutes, and the whole car shakes and rattles when the speedometer passes 50. And my twin brother, with whom I have been through so much since childhood, my brother the good twin, not so much fun as me the bad twin, and really quite dangerous – the CIA and an even worse Defense Department agency – in Southeast Asia in two periods when I was there on the other side. And up well into middle age, well after I became published, he was still sending me ads from a Washington paper for door-to-door salesman jobs or entry level jobs in grim business writing. He has been sending me classified ads like this for 30 years. And what if it should turn out he was right about me all along. And an ear-nose-throat doctor has just told me that the ringing in my ears is there because something is "asymmetrical," which calls for an MRI, and I know what that means.

I used to be able to lie in bed and my memory was so good I could put together whatever it was I had been doing on any day in the year.

I groan at the thought of every book or magazine article or pamphlet or web article about how to overcome insomnia. Very light exercise before sleep. Use the bed only for sleeping! Tighten and release your head muscles, then neck, then shoulders, down to the tips of your toes. Take a hot bath. Have a snack, but not too much. Rid your life of caffeine. Go to bed at exactly the same time every night. Keep the window open. Always keep it shut. Use something from nature – valerian or melatonin or L-tryptophan or a homeopathic concoction. And nothing works. Nothing.

Everything in life open ended. Cathy, whom I loved, then Vannie, whom I loved, then Judy, whom I loved, then Bonnie, whom I loved, and my first wives, Anne and Brenda, loved them too, and then more of the might-have-beens – Tina, the girl with net stockings, the pretty freedom fighter in Nicaragua, and on and on and then all the way back to earliest times, to Sandie, and most of all to Kitty. I could stay up all night dreaming of Kitty in that time when I was 15 and it looked for the first time that life would work out. And I had stayed up dreaming erotic dreams of her again when we were in touch by phone when I was 50.

And now I think of a recent betrayal – an attempted hijacking of a foreign workshop we had spent a year setting up, this betrayal staged by a malevolent drunk singer, whom I had trusted, and a greedy southern Italian businesswoman who is not what she seems.

I wonder now if anyone but me has noticed that those giveaway pamphlets about how to sleep that you sometimes see in doctors' offices are produced by drug companies that sell sleeping pills. Certainly everyone has noticed that a good percentage of the anti-smoking TV ads are produced by Phillip Morris, a company whose life depends upon people being addicted young to nicotine, and that the most visible ads for moderate drinking come from Budweiser.

I am feeling coldly logical now. Something is falling into place that should go into the book on writing I am writing. It goes like this: If the pill companies have an interest in promoting insomnia, and the cigarette companies in seeing that nicotine addiction flourishes, and Budweiser needs binge drinking for its bottom line, what about the hidden motives of the owners of writers' magazines and publishers of how-to-write books who say all writers should sit for three hours a day in front of computer screens even when the screens are blank? Or that everything will be fine once you learn to use hooks and epiphanies and closures in all your stories.

I toss and I turn, trying one side and then the other. In my mind I see steel shelves at Barnes & Noble holding books with advice on how to write and how to overcome writer's block. They must weigh a ton. You could get killed if they fell on you.

family horror

In another of our workshops I flashed on Olivier's Hamlet, which had come out 35 years before, way back when I was 15 and moving between those Georgian buildings in that lake country boarding school well away from the family, well away from both Connecticut and the White Mountains. Seeing for myself worlds without family filters. And one of them was Hamlet's world, and the last scenes in Hamlet made complete sense to me – the stage littered with bodies – how could it be any other way?

And now 35 years later in new worlds in this new time presenting themselves to me – 35 years and it feeling that suddenly my life was opening up, feeling I could go anywhere now, the memories of that boarding school time came flooding in – that this was the real time for me, the family time being a dark diversion – which was something I was not clear on until I wrote about it.

And now in my psyche there was a stage again on which bodies were strewn. And it seemed as natural as the killings at the end of Hamlet. And I wondered that such a time of killing, between boarding school and now, could ever have surprised me.

Cousin Margaret's head had turned blue and swelled up like an athletic ball on the respirator and she had just died of leukemia despite what had seemed a successful bone marrow transplant – and they blamed the leukemia on her disobedient way of life, and she'd said at the end that because of that she wanted to die, and she had talked about things her father, and mother too, had done to her. And suddenly our gorgeous young Cousin Deirdre was back in New Hampshire, just out of a Minnesota battered women's shelter and her mother blamed her for it on grounds she was too pretty, and the mother said she really kind of liked the guy who did it. And it turned out this was not for the first time, and Deirdre was in tentative treatment for trauma now for it came to light that from the ages of seven to sixteen, until he died in a motorcycle accident that carried hints of suicide, her brother, my Cousin Paul, had fucked her nearly every day, penetration as soon as she was large enough, and beat her so that her mother had commented on the welts on her back, and Deirdre, Paul and her older brother and her mother had all been living on top of each other in small "flats" in London and New York, and, all but the broher, at the end in a small mill town house in New Hampshire.

And now out in San Diego our cousin by marriage, a sparkling young woman named Elka, hung herself. And near the same time it was revealed through my mother that my brother Peter had been in the Philippines with the recently enlarged Reagan-time CIA. In Manila, where I had been with the anti-American opposition and under death threat, and where others I knew were wanted men who were being assassinated by government thugs.

And everything in the past was in question now that for the first time since adolescence I had started paying close attention to the places I came from and to that sometimes accomplished, sometime unintentionally comic, often unbending, sometimes kind, apparently safely neo-Victorian family.

When I was six, Gaga had given a radio address about why America should get into the war in support of our natural friends, the English.

At the end of the talk – I know this because a copy was given to me by my grandmother Nana when I was 15 and old enough to appreciate it – at the end Gaga said that just the week before he had gotten word that his son-in-law Rob, whom he thought of as his son, he said, had gone down in flames fighting the Germans.

It was decades before I, or even Uncle Rob's son, learned that he actually died when he and an RAF cadet friend climbed a fence after the pubs closed and broke into an RAF training field, started up a flimsy single-engine trainer, took off and crashed it – dying not, as in the family version of reality, in action in the Battle of Britain, but rather in a fatal drunken flying accident.

And I understand that they are still – to this day – passing copies of Gaga's war speech down through the generations.

Orderly Strangulation

In debating, the judges were always making notes, making sure you were consistent, making sure that you not only had good points of your own that you could back up but also that you could ably handle all points made by your opponents. When I got up to speak – whether in an Anglophile prep school or before a Rotary Club or in a bare bones rural high school – I would begin by introducing what I was going to say. I would list the items, saying that now I am going to say "1… 2… 3…." Then I would go through each item, "1… 2… 3…" – bringing in statistics and a few quotes – which I would get from my frequently updated card file of quotes and statistics that I had on hand for any eventuality. My newly baritone-bass voice would soar as I went along. Then at the end I would note, calmly if triumphantly, that I had thoroughly taken care of "1… 2… 3…."

I was exalting logic, linear thinking, deductive reasoning, and leaving no room for induction, intuition, unfolding. I was, though I did not know it at the time, right in the tradition that began with the art-hating Greek philosophers that still dominates in the Western academic world.

There were some glorious moments in my young days in New

Hampshire when I used debating to get out of the box in which family and school had placed me. But I suspected it was not glorious to knock the life out of important subjects – this way of approaching a subject so that there would be no loose ends, no room for the opposing side to breathe, no way out.

Whatever the subject under debate, it was no longer a living subject that could grow and take surprising directions. I had successfully contained it. "1... 2... 3...." And so I would return to my boarding school with our latest trophy – topped by another bronze woman, holding high a laurel wreath, this naked bronze girl who would tower over the much more modest sports trophies in the school's trophy case.

Meanwhile, I got my top grades by excelling in writing answers to essay exam questions and in doing term papers that followed the debate formula. An introduction saying I will say "1... 2... 3...." Then the body of the work in which I say "1... 2... 3...." And then the conclusion in which I say I have said "1... 2... 3...."

Many years later when I was teaching, to my surprise, a college course, English 101, inside a northern Catskills high school, this old "1... 2... 3..." stuff was just what a hectoring high school principal and a pompous English Department chairman tried in vain to get me to have students do over and over again – those old straight-jacketed research papers that are so honored in academe. I found with these students, who seemed to me much brighter than the principal or the chairman, what I had found with myself so many years back when I was a big debater. I found that with these kids in the Catskills, as it had been with me way back in New Hampshire, it was easy to do winning papers and exam essays if you were ready to falsify something complicated by giving the illusion of wrapping it up neatly. And I found they craved much more. So I got out of the way of what they really wanted and needed to write.

That principal and that English chairman told me in memos how important it was to falsify in this "1... 2... 3..." way as preparation for college. This was another sad truth, and made me remember how deadly, and easy, college writing had been.

For I had found at college that if I was uninterested in a class – as I usually was – I could still figure out what was wanted and scrape by with winning logic, even when unprepared – a little like the way I did it when I was winning debates whether or not I believed in the side I was taking. And very much like my last year in boarding school when I had lost interest and went into debates unprepared, but kept to the linear forms and won anyway.

Back in New Hampshire in the years I prepared thoroughly I had made convincing cases that world government was the wave of the future, which I hoped, and that world government was a foreign idea to bring America down, which I found a contemptible proposition. I argued for universal health care, which seemed an obviously good thing to me, and did just as well if not better when I argued against it, citing really dumb ideas about free enterprise that gullible people swallowed.

I would hate for students to lose such a useful tool as silly linear logic for dealing with silly or malevolent professors. Just as I would hate to have them give up the practice, which is sometimes needed to placate professors, of throwing in a lot of extraneous footnotes. The footnotes, however, are not as valued as the "1… 2… 3…" system. If you get a particularly insular and rigid and maybe bigoted professor, often all you have to do is put his bigoted opinions in "1… 2… 3…" form and hand them back to him.

I wondered how real professors could keep on reading this awful, linear, unneeded writing. Maybe it is because so many of them are numb from having to write and publish similar nonsense in their little-read academic journals in order to get tenure – and remain so frightened afterwards that they still feel they have to do it.

Not me. I was teaching as an underpaid auxiliary professor – operating as if underground, disguised as a professor, doing it because my finances were in such disarray that a bank was about to seize my house. But I had already started the Authentic Writing Workshops. I was not going to do any of the things professors are scared into doing. I was hardly laying the groundwork for an academic career. And anyway the money wasn't much.

I decided I would strive for honesty in this faux academic career, and make up for the times I had been dishonest by writing to order when I was living on freelance work.

sense of triumph

I looked around the big meeting room in Livermore Hall – folding chairs lined up with leather sofas – and realized more than half of this small boarding school's students, maybe 50 boys and also eight faculty members, were here. Such a crowd, it seemed, that I might have been speaking in a coliseum. And for all I knew they were as bloodthirsty as crowds at the ancient world's deadly Roman games.

I knew this room well for this was where we assembled to hear outside speakers – some of them silly, like a burly man who was to give an anti-Communism talk but wound up doing card tricks – and some were deadly serious, like a tall, thin Quaker who knew what was what in China, including that Mao was popular and would win and Chiang Kai-shek was a discredited warlord that Harry Truman should not be supporting. But now I myself was about to speak here, leading off for the affirmative side on whether our government should provide free health care and higher education. I was 15. My voice had not finished changing. A year earlier I had been considered the dumbest kid in the school and was treated that way by everyone except a key teacher – we called them masters – and two guys who had become my friends in spite of how I had been so slow and unpopular. "Speedy."

But by the time I was poised to speak in Livermore I had, suddenly, and mysteriously, risen right to the top of my class. I had just made the varsity debate team though I was two years younger than even the brightest varsity debaters in other years.

The room was so familiar. Not just for speakers but also as the place the whole school gathered after dinner every night to sing a hymn and hear a prayer. On the walls were murals showing this rolling-hill part of New Hampshire in autumn colors with figures of the future thrown in – a streamlined train and an airplane with four propellers and nautical-style portholes.

Often that year and the next two years I would be standing in this room surrounded by these gentle murals, building up my case, demolishing my opponents, all the while practicing careful eye contact, my oratory soaring to the point where at moments it was as if I could own the room. That's how it felt. My words covering over the hymns and prayers that had been said or sung here – this meeting room across a hall from a smaller meeting room where mail was handed out in the morning – where now I would almost always find a scented letter in a pastel envelope from Sandie, who like me was 15, an hour away in our sister school, St. Mary's-in-the-Mountains – the envelope's stamp, as on my letters to her, upside down to show the writer was so distracted by love it was not possible to get things right side up – and on the back of the envelope in capital letters, S.W.A.K., which according to custom stood for "Sealed With A Kiss" – something far beyond anything I had thought could happen to me – for less than a year ago I had been the slowest, most unpopular boy in this school, "Speedy" – me the slow and bad twin, in the same class here with Peter, the smart, good twin – and by some miracle I had drawn even and, I believed, I was passing him. At one moment I'd been flunking my courses, the next I'd shot to the top of the class, and met Sandie – a girlfriend! – just as I became a member of this varsity debate team.

I was finally seen as bright. Not popular yet, still often ostracized, but not totally despised – and now here I was, on the spot in this familiar room filled with boys and masters lined up on folding chairs

– standing before them – and I had to make the opening speech. Could I carry it off with a voice that was still changing, a voice that had recently gone from alto to baritone and might still crack as it headed down to bass? And would I be ridiculed and ostracized even further for presuming that I could get away with it?

Right in front of me were the judges. Mrs. Homer, a woman with a pretty monkey face who was the mother of my confident-seeming classmate Bob Homer and also president of the League of Women Voters in the nearby town of Plymouth – she and two other Plymouth League of Women Voters women, these three to judge this debate that would begin the moment I opened my mouth – if I could open my mouth.

Behind me at our table was my debate colleague and new best friend Ken Kaplan, who was a sixth former, the equivalent of senior, while I was just a fourth former. And at the other table behind me was the Portland, Maine team – Lois and Michael – who last year had carried back to Portland some major debating trophies. These two – the legendary Lois, a beautiful, stately girl who was black in mostly white northern New England, though you forgot that fast, and sturdy Michael – the New England debating champions, coached by a craggy man named Mr. Walsh who produced a handbook on each year's national subject that went out to debaters all over America. The strongest team in New England, and their famous coach too, right here in this room where I was in front of this crowd at this school of mine where I still might be an outcast.

Me – a fourth former – Speedy – lucky to be where I was, lucky to have a girlfriend who necked on those rare occasions we got up to her school or they got down to ours – it all being almost as if I were one of the popular guys. And now my life hinged on this moment in this familiar room with the fall foliage murals where, my mouth dry, I did begin to speak even while remembering that I was the slow, dumb, shy guy who would not know what to say.

Very early on the morning after my victory – we'd won and the League of Women Voters women had named me Best Speaker – I and all the school debaters on all levels were off in a school van with our coach to a practice tournament at a southern New Hampshire high school. No one was calling me Speedy today.

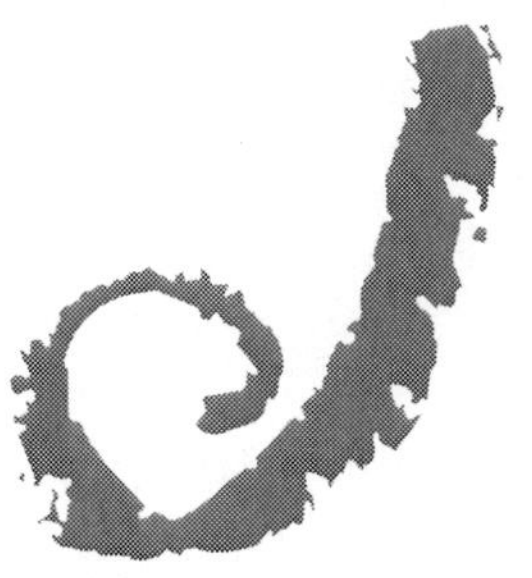

payoff

In the beginning, when I was still shy, and speaking hesitantly, and not winning as often as I thought I could. But suave Dmitri Nabokov, who would later become my debate partner, took me aside, in an act of great kindness, and pointed out that I did not need to worry about performing badly in these outlying towns since no one who saw me in practice debates in small New Hampshire high schools was likely to ever see me again. I should just speak right out, he said. I should keep in mind that I had nothing to lose.

So I started booming out my arguments at these practice debates. My voice suddenly stopped cracking. It really was moving down into baritone and towards bass. To my surprise, people told me it was resonate like a radio announcer's. Me, 15, the weakling outcast. Suddenly I was winning.

Moreover, debating took me inside our sister school, St. Mary's-in-the-Mountains. Four of us were driven up there late one afternoon by our English teacher and debate coach, Joe Abbey, so we could stage a debate for the St. Mary's girls. Their English teacher, who had nice breasts and wore fluffy sweaters, was considering starting a debate team with the girls. The rumor was that she was dating Joe.

The debate went well – here in this soft feminine place. As well as my debates were going in raw-bone high school rooms. We came, and we orated, and we had sandwiches and cocoa, but we left without any one-on-one contact with any of the girls. Though I did notice during the debate that a brown-eyed girl was looking my way even when I was not speaking.

Two months later, I went along in freezing cold in a school van full of farts and punches to an early Sunday evening dance up at St. Mary's, which was in the White Mountains, where mysteriously in the summers I was as popular as I was unpopular the rest of the year in school.

St. Mary's, now in this northern winter, feels like a warm place. The room where they have the dance is all soft colors and gentle lights – not at all like our school's place for rare social gatherings, which is a room in Livermore Hall where there is a cold linoleum floor, harsh lights and black leather chairs.

Now, from one end of this girl-like room at St. Mary's we boys burst in from the cold. And we see at the other end these girls in girl clothes, some, like Joe's teacher friend, with soft sweaters that follow their girl shapes, including, sometimes, as with Joe's friend, actual breasts. It is art and it is poetry and it is music!

But I might have been crossing a dangerous mountain pass to get to that end of the room where the girls were standing, looking unconcerned – where this girl was standing. Smiling. Brown hair and brown eyes. Chubby, which was okay. Actually nice. Big sad eyes that she turned to me and then averted. White teeth. The girl who had watched me so closely during the debate.

She asked me to dance. That was the way it was done here. The girls would do the asking the first time around here on their home ground.

She came over and said, "My name is Sandie." I said, "I'm Fred." She said, "Would you dance with me?" Otherwise, we did not speak. I followed her out to the dance floor area, which seemed suddenly a really glamorous place though it was just the floor of St. Mary's big lounge room with the tables pushed back.

It quickly became clear that this girl with the averted eyes and the new breasts knew things people like us had to learn outside the formal white-glove dancing classes to which parents like ours had sent us on Friday evenings back in Connecticut.

Without conversation now, my outstretched left arm and her outstretched right arm gave way at precisely the same time. Her right hand, which had no glove on it, was now turned and cupped in my left hand against my school blazer shoulder. My right hand was way out of dancing-class position, way down her soft back. Our bodies were together – and this "cheek to cheek" thing began, me leaning down and she pulling herself up. And the fingers of her left hand, oh God, touched the back of my neck. And as we swayed, her leg went between mine and pressed against me.

The next week I overheard one of the popular athletes say, "Speedy's in love.... Speedy has a pig.... The girl who necked with Marty last year." But I was becoming just confident enough now to see at least a small element of jealousy. For it was rare now that they used that nickname "Speedy" that had haunted me until I began to seem a winner.

I saw Sandie again when there was a joint Holderness-St. Mary's glee club concert at Plymouth State Teachers College. It seemed magical, though I had to watch from the back of the darkened hall because the Holderness glee club director, Mr. English, had rejected me. But I did speak to Sandie and invited her down to our spring dance weekend, which was one of only three such Holderness weekends with girls each school year.

For the moment I had stopped thinking about my debating career. Sandie and I now were in the old school gym, which had been decorated with blue and silver-like bunting, our school colors. All the boys were in dinner jackets, rented from a place on the edge of Plymouth across from a shoe-tree factory, and all the girls were in formal gowns. The girls all had gardenia corsages, which had been given out at the door. The smell of gardenias overwhelmed the usual fart and sweat smells of the gym.

And here I was with Sandie for a second time. This time Sandie was in a dress held up by what looked to be flimsy strings. Her leg was between my legs again, her leg frankly against my hard penis – my hand now sliding down her partially bare back, her fingers linked at my neck – her gown such that when I drew back just enough to look down as we swayed it was easy to imagine my real life had begun and I was with an actual naked woman. I was a very long way away from cold hard debater's facts.

But it seemed certain to me that without debating I would not be in this position. With cold logic, I attributed Sandie to my increasing success with cold logic in debating.

Debating was taking me out of that hollow shell in which I had felt trapped all my life, and Sandie, it seemed, had been waiting for me outside the shell. It really seemed like it was my ability to be coldly logical that got me here.

the story changes

I go into these stories again and again, which is necessary if you are suspicious of pat endings.

As I keep writing about it now I tell of how I also found a girlfriend, not Sandie now but Kitty, who made me the envy of even the dull athletes. And I write of how in that summer abroad, back with the family again, after all that had happened with girls and debate trophies, it seemed I had gone nowhere, my twin was at the center still and again. My mother's mother, who was with us, had said my debate triumphs were all very well but maybe it would have been different if Peter had put the same effort into it and then he, not Fred, would be the best debater in New England. And how strange, they said, that Fred has this pretty new girlfriend Kitty. Peter should have been seen as such a catch. When I picked up Kitty's letters at American Express offices in Paris and Venice they laughed at me – Fred presuming to have this loving girlfriend he did not deserve.

When decades later I finally began writing seriously about youth, I wrote and rewrote about how I would wander on my own in Paris. It was a stimulating walk alone through the grand-scale Place de la Concorde from our hotel on Rue St. Honoré to the Jeu de Paume, which was where the Impressionists were. The Impressionists, whom I had never heard of before that summer abroad. I had never thought much about art beyond *Saturday Evening Post* covers and the Varga girls in *Esquire*, although that summer I did draw with charcoal, along with Peter, from a café across from the Opera. I drew even though the art teacher at Holderness said I was the logical one, the one who used prose in his speeches while Peter leaned towards poetry – just as if I did not have Keats and Wordsworth and Wolfe and Conrad as my private advisers then as I now in this summer suddenly had Manet and Monet and Renoir and van Gogh, and Gaugin and his South Seas dreams that went beyond even Conrad.

It was my mother who first took us to see the Impressionists – which she knew from long ago when she spent her junior year from Smith abroad. But otherwise these painters were outside any context I knew. There was nothing like this on the walls at school or at home in Connecticut, or in my paternal grandparents' grand houses in the White Mountains. Neither my mother nor any of my elders had before this ever even talked to me about art.

Sometimes now in Paris I would go off to a theater I discovered on the busy Right Bank Rue des Capuchins where, though only 16 and looking younger, I could see actual naked girls proudly dancing. Smiling. One of them reaching out a hand to a boyfriend in the wings. And this did not seem inconsistent with my going again and again to the Jeu de Paume.

Writing about it years later I am right there looking at Renoir's girl on a swing who seems to be a girl for me whom I have encountered on a path. I am right there again, and I still see every wall of the museum and still have in my head the precise location of each painting – the exact location still the same for me, though they were later moved to a bigger museum building. I am still standing before Monet's rows of hay stacks and rows of poplars in shifting light and his various aspects of Chartres and the Houses of Parliament – and I am in the South Seas with Gaugin as far from New Hampshire as you can get, but no farther than where van Gogh takes me to places right here in France. And then

Manet, that wonderful girl Olympia on her back on the bed. I still know just where Olympia is. And I know that in the far end of the next room, if I look up and to the left, there will be those picnicking artists again with their stately nude model. My eyes are open.

Writing about that summer, I then come to my return and my last year, sixth form year, at school when I again won big debating championships, and had top grades, but did it by bluff now, my reputation such that if the judges saw I was unprepared they would not trust what they saw and would vote for my side anyway. And the masters, who graded my slickly logical papers for classes (other than English where I did not bluff), could not get the conception that I had stopped doing the reading. In this time when I also walked away from my deepest interests of the mind and heart.

I write again and again about this time in Paris and my last year in school to understand what had happened when I was back trapped in the place where I had begun, those Georgian buildings in the lake country where, although my life had expanded, it now, as the end drew near, seemed in new ways precarious and empty, almost like when I first arrived as the despised "Speedy," the bad twin overshadowed by the good twin. On the surface it must have seemed to the boys and the masters that I was still riding high. But in my last year, under the surface, I was encountering bleakness and confusion. I even walked away from my love and my muse, Kitty – life after Paris had become that bleak and confusing.

But as I keep going back into the story the emphasis shifts, for the paintings appear in full color. I would not admit it yet when I was 16, but art had all of a sudden dismantled my passion for logic.

As I write now, going back into the story again and again as any serious writer must, it is not just that I had been thrown back into a suffocating place with the parents and grandmother and good-boy brother, thrown back into my old sad place in the world. As I write I spend more time each time with the paintings. The paintings that so moved me that I knew there was something more breathtaking and magnificent in art than there had ever been in this carefully constructed life I had put togther in order to make myself something other than Speedy. I knew it from Keats and Wordsworth, who had given me hope and pleasure, but because I could write I had the temerity to compartmentalize them. I knew it from the beauty of the mountains and the love of Kitty, though I had still been able to detour around affections when my debating skills were on the line.

In Paris, however, those paintings hit me where I had no defenses.

I wanted art, I knew now I needed art, but I also knew that logic, the opposite of art, was where I had found my safety. So I desperately hoped I could somehow hold on to the constructions that had seemed so sound when only in my head. It was as if there would be nothing to live for if constructions that had satisfied till now failed me.

And so as I write about it many years later, going back into the story for the 100th time, what takes over is the paintings I saw that summer – far more than the limits of family.

What happened was something I could not quite make my own yet. But it never went away. The paintings in Paris that opened up something almost unbearably fine. And which in a wonderfully non-linear way were a part of the origins of what in another era and another art form would become the Authentic Writing Workshops.

II

the end of life

I was suddenly in that place, Princeton, where nothing I loved – except for pretty girls who in prep school fashion appeared only on certain weekends in this gray male bastion – nothing I loved was honored much. The air was not filled with poetry and music. Debating was something for social rejects. The student paper that year liked Eisenhower. No one, it seemed, openly wrote or painted, and singing meant football songs or trite close harmony by small preppy groups. Most students were little old Republicans in their politics. And usually drunk. As was I – not the Republican part. The English professors stressed cold analysis and went to enormous lengths to kill off any reason for being moved by literature. The fake Oxford-Cambridge Gothic buildings had all the discomfort of England and none of the charm. English-style casement windows that let in the cold air, creating that subtle British combination of being stuffy and chilly at the same time. On the surface, Harris tweed and Oxford gray flannel. Below the surface, communal basement lavatories and showers with mildew and slippery floors that never dried, and for meals the undergraduate "commons" where the meat was blue when it was not green.

Then in an otherwise not very interesting freshman English class

I read a portion of the autobiography of John Stuart Mill from an anthology you had to buy that was edited by the young professor who taught the course. It seemed at first a happy story.

Mill had succeeded when ridiculously young in doing what I even now, in the face of malaise and paralysis, still hoped to do – get everything in its place. His father was James Mill, an influential political philosopher in the early 19TH century. The elder Mill and his best friend, the more renowned political philosopher Jeremy Bentham, decided they would home school the boy, using all the progressive ideas they had developed about education.

Bentham and the older Mill were the creators and chief proponents of what was called Utilitarianism and they and their followers were known as utilitarians. It seemed to me as I read about it the perfect vessel to contain all that might be good in the world. It seemed to me the sort of idea that had saved me when I was a weak and ridiculed adolescent, apparently doomed forever to be an object of schoolboy sadism.

Their central idea was that all action should be directed towards achieving the greatest good – in 19TH-century language they called it "the greatest happiness" – for the greatest number of people. They looked to the utility of any action or plan or program, which meant always keeping in mind this idea of the greatest happiness for the greatest number. And they were leading increasingly successful fights in Parliament to, among much else, get rid of child labor in mines and factories, clean up the open sewers that ran through city streets, stop the widespread executions carried out in England for small financial crimes.

Just like me, I thought, a 16-year-old socialist and pacifist coming out of the most unlikely place, New Hampshire. So very much like me, this John Stuart Mill, a voice calling for justice, and actually getting recognized – like me, the New England debating champion.

I read on. Just as the Utilitarians thought social conditions could be improved, so did they believe that education could be revolutionized. And Bentham and James Mill decided they would prove their theories by taking over the education of James' son, who would be home schooled.

I had learned to read late, taught by my mother because I could make no sense of school. But otherwise my education had been entrusted to institutions. I read now John Stuart Mill's account of how, though he never thought of himself as being particularly brilliant, his father and Bentham never pushed lessons that did not interest him; they helped him follow up his interests, and let him drop or postpone what bored him. Young John could read classical Greek by the time he was three. By the time he was eight he had mastered the Greek and Roman classics and all important historical literature. By the time he was 12 he had added economics, philosophy and mathematics. He also learned all the main modern European languages, and covered all the principal works of literature, as well as the science of the day. While still a teenager he was writing and publishing learned articles. He himself had become an important leader in the thriving Utilitarian movement by the time he reached 20. Just like what I had wanted to be.

Then it all fell apart – rather like, it seemed now, the new life I had built up had all fallen apart in my final year at school, the year before entering this intensely unsympathetic, ivy-strangled college. How like me, Mill coming to the end of the road. And how awful that the reasons he gave seemed so clear.

For now my heart sank as I read about what he called his crisis. At the very time he was on top of the world, he asked himself if everything he wanted, all the changes in laws and institutions and education and politics, everything to which he looked forward, suddenly became just what he wanted would this be "a great joy and happiness?" And he found he had to answer no. And he knew he had nothing left to live for.

This knowledge of what lay so close to the surface stayed with me for decades. And it seemed yet another reason explaining why all I had achieved in ambition-fueled prep school days had come to seem so minor that in my last year I had walked away from everything good in my life.

I did not feel my life was over. And in fact there was some real happiness and a great deal of excitement, not just depression, in the years ahead. But it all felt fragile. Immediately I was in a dark, intense depression, fueled by the alcohol that was so much a part of this university's identity.

What happened immediately would in another setting have been called a nervous breakdown, as would what happened to Mill if the context had been different. A nervous breakdown, with suicidal overtones. What hit me hardest was how little joy I would get if all the political reform I wanted came to pass – and so how little right now I had to live for.

I did not look at the autobiography again for 30 years. One afternoon I had gone, just before a class at the Art Students League, to my local library in Chelsea to look up the painter Joan Miro, whom I was coming to admire. I wasn't reading much about art but I was doing an amazing amount of looking, night and day, in museums and galleries, and then for a year and a half in studios in every art school in town and many private drawing sessions, starting my day early at the League and ending it around midnight drawing models in a Soho basement.

For some reason I had been thinking about Miro, and wondering if I were wrong that Miro was a man, since the first name was Joan. One of those small nagging things that get into your head. So I went to the "Mi" pages in Collier's Encyclopedia, and by mistake opened to the John Stuart Mill entry.

And I read now what I must have read in the past without it registering of how in his dark suicidal period Mill began to see that happiness was not, as he had been taught, something you could get by going after what you thought you wanted directly. It had to be a byproduct of something more. And he sensed what that something more would be, and so, as the encyclopedia writer put it, he set out to revive his "atrophied emotions."

He was drawn for the first time to poetry for pleasure, not to complete an education. He was drawn especially to the Romantics. And he was drawn into nature not for botanical and biological studies but for the pleasure of it. And so too he was now drawn to painting and to music.

And this made all the dfference. As one day it would for me too.

5 professors

This gray, reactionary, intensely alcoholic and snobbish place where those in power frequently tried to ape what they saw as their betters in England, where everyone spoke in the way certain upper-class Americans spoke. Physically, it was a Disneyland version of 800-year-old Oxbridge buildings set down in New Jersey. Across Nassau Street there was a more American stage set, a Williamsburg sort of town – uniform buildings of plastic-looking red brick with white pillars.

There on Nassau Street you could buy white bucks and Oxford gray suits and leather-covered flasks to take to football games, but no books and no art supplies. Back behind the Williamsburg façade the place was as segregated as if this were Alabama – narrow streets behind Nassau Street filled with black people, many of whom worked at the college and in the eating clubs, which were Princeton's version of fraternities. The presence of black servants was often given as the reason most of the clubs would not take black students as members – though by the time I got there things had opened up to the point where each class had an actual Negro in it. They had to be kept out of the better clubs, it was said, not because the college men were bigoted but because, club officers claimed, the loyal Negroes doing the serving would be the first to object to integration.

The English department was full of celebrated experts on modern American literature who seemed to hate literature – the Frost expert who wrote a book about how Robert Frost was only a minor poet and, worse, no gentleman; the Hemingway expert whom Hemingway said should be avoided; the Melville expert who wrote a book about how this Moby Dick was a homoerotic treatise, celebrating the joy of sinking your fist into white blubber.

I wrote a column in the *Daily Princetonian* – assigning it to myself since I was editorial chairman (something I did in the free time I had created by not going to classes) – a column saying these English professors had no feel for writing, for anything aesthetic or moving – mentioning their claims heard so often in class that there were right and wrong answers about the meaning of any given work of literature, that you could really understand a novel if you saw one of their blackboard outlines of it – their unspoken claim that literature was a dry subject where emotion had no place. I said in my *Princetonian* column that all this awful stuff was light years away from the experience of walking along the green banks of Princeton's Carnegie Lake in springtime – an experience foreign to these tweedy professors.

Carlos Baker, the Hemingway expert, was the English Department chairman (gender always specific at this place back then when women were never seen except when dates came down on some weekends). Carlos Baker called a special meeting of all the preceptors (the Anglo term for instructors, such British-sounding terms favored here the same way fake Gothic architecture was favored). He gave them talking points to refute this young Fred Poole person – for how can you know anything about literature if you do not follow those who so bravely analyze it and analyze and analyze it. Then he clinched his argument by showing them the transcript of my grades, which I thought were not bad considering I spent most of my time away from the campus and hardly ever went to classes and still managed to pass sometimes – but which he thought would be the clincher that would prevent Fred Poole and anyone else who thought the way young Poole did from further corrupting the students. He told his preceptors to show copies of the transcript to everyone in their preceptorials, and then, I suppose, he went back to analyzing Hemingway.

Three of my classmates used the spring break that year to go to Cuba, which was then run by the father of our classmate Ruben Batista, who gave them gambling chips. They hid in the back of a van to get into the Hemingway place, and met Hemingway just as he was finishing his morning writing and starting his morning drinking. He invited them to join him. Many drinks later he sent them away telling them not to tell Carlos Baker about this. He wanted nothing to do with Carlos Baker.

on the run

It is very late on my first night out on the Christoforo Colombo and I am 20, nearing 21. The first light of dawn is coming. We are high up on the boat deck, where we have just been kissing, with a little of what back then was called "petting." This soft, intelligent, red-headed girl, who has already finished college, is saying she is glad she is on this summer trip because she fears her engagement to a proper young man back in Bronxville or some place like it was a horrible mistake.

So she takes off this ring – saying, when I met you tonight I knew I'd have to do this. She takes the ring and hurls it into the North Atlantic.

No! – fiction! – ring not over the rail. NO!

The ring was there – and it did feel like she had put me on the spot – saying that meeting me this night convinced her she would have to get rid of the ring – put me on the spot so firmly that she might have cast the ring into the North Atlantic in the course of our necking at the boat deck rail – necking as the Chistoforo Colombo was moving toward the South Atlantic. She might have thrown the ring.

But she didn't.

I see her as clearly as if it were just hours ago that the sky over the ocean, over us, was turning red with the dawn – actually a range of colors from hot orange to lukewarm purple – this dawn still so clear it could, this dawn, have been a just-passed dawn, not a dawn that was just-passed 50 years ago – her, the picture of her, with something of my own aspiration and my own suspicion of commitment in her, but still her, whom I can never really know, not me, whom I hope to know. And although I see her hand, just disentangled from me, held out – slightly pink, slightly freckled – to display the ring – her hand in memory soft and slightly scented – I do not, do not, do not, do not see the other hand disentangle and slide the ring off and hurl it into the ocean.

This is fiction.

This is me running from myself. This is me falsifying, like my literary enemies, so as to get the focus off myself, off what I know – me so filled with aspiration and – except for the effects of the night's Strega and the brandy – so unsure, at not quite 21, just feeling my way, though in favor in my mind of total immersion in the flow and life and sex and beauty and love and death and grandeur – but instead I am, then and when I wrote so much later, just putting a toe in – running into the coward's shelter – fiction!

For she does not take off the ring with the fingers of the other hand disentangled from me and she does not lean back while still in my arms and throw that ring into the ocean –

And although I wrote it I do not see, as I did in fiction, a diamond of a size so large and hence showy that it would signal my family, if they were somehow to see it, that she did not come from Our Kind of People. It makes a point, making the diamond that big, but it diminishes the story.

It helps me run from the story, from unbearable beauty and aspiration and fear of commitment, and the ever-present possibility of betrayal.

As I write I see her soft hair, her soft hand and her light eyes, and I smell the ocean and I remember her own scent, and I feel aroused by her that night – though I will not, that night, choose her over all others I seek – for this is not precisely the picture I seek – her skin lightly freckled, like mine, though unlike mine soft and lightly scented –

Though not shiny and clear and olive as in the fiction I write in my head and may turn into lies on paper – her skin not nearly Italian enough.

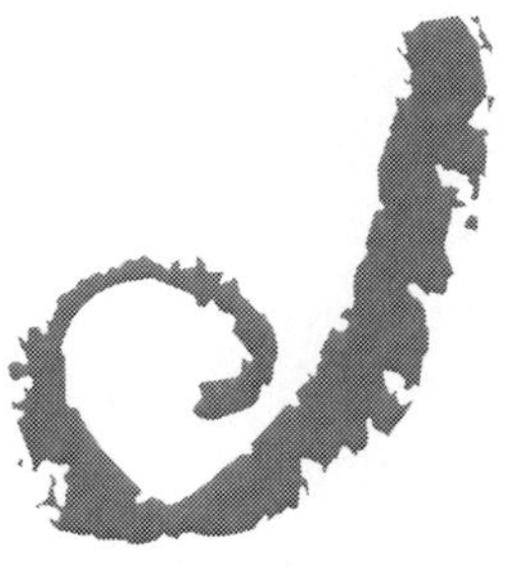

franny

When a literature professor at Princeton would put ten numbered sentences on a blackboard, almost no one would question aloud that this told you what a book meant, what it really meant. And the students sat there in their tweed sport coats or Oxford gray jackets, worn in uniform style with chinos, smoking Camels or Phillip Morris's, looking at the professor sometimes as if he were a boring fool and sometimes as if he might be taken seriously.

And so on an exam I could write a nonsense essay parroting back those ten points. It was not necessary to read the book. Reading the book could be a disadvantage, since real literature, like all real art, gets into mystery, and to these professors there was no mystery. I was so discouraged with them that I stopped taking English courses. But I was in a small minority. There were boys in my class who became the stars of the English department. They won the prizes for critical endeavors, and might parlay this nonsense into Rhodes Scholarships before entering the corporate world that was so honored at this gray place.

Would anyone ever understand what was wrong with these English professors? They were like the people Sinclair Lewis, who was one of the authors they considered passé, called "men of measured merriment," but they had power for they were the official critics of Lewis and so many more of their betters.

And then suddenly there was a ray of hope. And again the hope came from J.D. Salinger, whose *The Catcher in the Rye* had been so welcome when I was in boarding school. And now he had done it again with his new *New Yorker* magazine story *Franny.*

Franny, this warm and sexy and spiritually tormented and brilliantly empathetic girl. In the story she is coming from her women's college to a place which is surely this men's college that I am in. Coming for a visit, since no girls study and no women teach here. She is coming for a weekend, a goddamn football weekend. And Franny's date, who meets her at the train, is one of these English Department stars. He is talking on and on about the meaning of this book and that book and why that other book is deservedly out of style, and about how his life is a constant series of triumphs against people who have no feel for correct literary theory. He is the most awful boor, and to me he is all too familiar.

Franny starts to complain about her own gray academic literature teachers and their followers. And he dismisses her words as error. And Franny is feeling faint. Does faint. Throws up. Faints again. Which seems to me an appropriate reaction to her date and his world.

My twin brother at this time is in the city at Columbia. He is in a fraternity and his roommate is Lou Cornell who was at Taft when we were at Holderness. Lou was one of the people who gloated with me when *The Catcher in the Rye* arrived. And also Lou is part of our summer world – the Cornells and Pooles in their big formal houses in the White Mountains.

Lou has decided that he will not enter the family business. He is majoring in English at Columbia. He plans to be an English professor.

I called Peter to express enthusiasm about the Salinger story *Franny* and Peter was strict with me on the phone. He said I obviously had misread it. What was clearly happening in the story, he said, was that Franny was pregnant. Her reaction to correct English department people had nothing to do with it. That was just my imagination. And far more important to both Peter Poole and Lou Cornell was that Lou's mother, Mary Cornell, a formidable woman in our summer community, had already pronounced upon it. There was family authority behind the she's-pregnant explanation. So, Peter was letting me know, English departments had nothing to fear, and neither did Pooles and Cornells – for a summer colony matriarch had certified Franny's pregnancy and thereby dismissed her heretical views.

The lines back then between warring worlds in family and school could be exceedingly thin.

(Years later Salinger, who almost never went public on anything, issued a public statement that Franny was not pregnant.)

betrothal

I return again and again to that summer in 1951 with the Impressionists in Paris, after which I lived on bluff, for my world had fallen apart. And when everything started to change again three and a half decades later I found my life in transformation once more in museum rooms, as I had in Paris. And again while lying in bed at night I could walk through such rooms and see everything that was on every wall – mostly in bigger museums this time, but much the same thing as in 1951. Hobbema's dark forest next to Constables' white horse on one wall of the Frick, Rembrandt's self portrait and his Polish Rider across the way – like in Paris with Renoir's pretty girl in frills on a swing on one wall, and on another remembered wall Manet's Olympia, clad only in a black choker.

Stepping into paintings, like stepping into a story. I began again one morning when I woke up in my small but light-filled one-bedroom Chelsea apartment with a tall, sweet-faced woman younger than me named Bonnie, the same name of that girl in Thailand. I had met this new Bonnie recently in an Adult Children of Alcoholics meeting – which was something I was doing that until now would have seemed hopelessly out of character. I had turned my answering machine off before she arrived. We lay together on the floor before moving to the bed. When in the night I heard the sound of the mechanical, though not the turned-off, audio part moving I was convinced it was my brother calling to say my mother was dying and I would have to go to a dread town in Florida to take charge. Me, who was not ruled by family. There was no such call from my brother, though I knew there might have been. The actual call on the machine turned out to be from a guy who, like me not long before, had split with his wife. He was wondering if he could sleep for a time in my living room.

Bonnie and I went up to the Met that morning. She had a Walkman, something new to me, but not to many by the mid-eighties. We passed it back and forth in the E and number 6 trains. Mozart on the subway. From 86TH and Lex we walked over to the Metropolitan. "Let's go up to the Met," I had said, it seeming a properly romantic move since I would be showing her a crucial part of what I thought of, with at this point perhaps insubstantial evidence, as myself.

I felt better than I had felt for years. I was silently thanking someone or something for the fact that I could have yet another adventure like this in this new time when everything was changing . We walked with arms around each other's waists, something I knew a lot about from 30 years back. In the museum I was going to show her my favorite paintings. What I found instead was how very narrow my scope was.

I had always, ever since Paris, gone to museums, or so I thought. I realized on this morning that it had been five years or more since I had been in a museum or a gallery. And I realized that I had not really been a constant museum goer since my first time in New York when my first New York girlfriend, Vannie, who wore black tights with heart-breaking style, had been an action painter. That was at the end of the fifties and the start of the sixties, a few crucial years after my time in the Jeu de Paume, years that had spanned college, the army, adventure in Haiti and Cuba, and a rapid career in wire service journalism.

Now in this new present I led Bonnie to the Impressionists. I don't know if she saw I was intensely embarrassed. I was uncomfortable because I did not know where the 19TH-century paintings were hung even though I had told her how important 19th-century paintings were to me. I asked a guard, just like an out-of-touch tourist would, and we found the Impressionists. And then we went to see the Rembrandts, since I knew Rembrandt from another teenage summer, one that I had spent in Holland. Then I tried to find the Hoppers. I knew Hopper from when I was 21 and a journalist in Indianapolis and roaming Chicago on weekends. I would look in on the Art Institute – where I became fixated upon *The Night Hawks*, that intense and lonely late night diner scene which I did not know was famous but did know it said everything I had wanted to say about loneliness and longing and fragile hope in seedy but alluring towns.

There were no Hoppers on display at the Met in 1986. And I had nothing else to show Bonnie. It did not occur to me to ask what she wanted to see. I was hit hard by the admission to myself that I knew so little, did not know what was meant by the High Middle Ages or the High Renaissance, had no idea of what a Rafael or Fra Angelico or a Donatello would look like, and I did not know their places in time. I loved art, but I did not know what I loved.

A few days later I was walking uptown from a dentist's office on 57th Street. On the radio while he was filling a cavity there had been bulletins about the space shuttle explosion that had just taken place – the space shuttle that carried an appealing woman who was really a New Hampshire schoolteacher. When I was on Madison nearing 75th street I saw I was passing the Whitney. Rather, I saw the Whitney had its own building, and had probably had it since some point in the early sixties when I had last seen it in its old small home, which you entered from the Museum of Modern Art. Now it had this big but gentle reddish modern building that for some reason was new to me. And inside I was suddenly listening to a happy old man who said he was a retired banker and was here as a volunteer docent. I followed him, though I had spent most of my life traveling and had always managed to avoid tour guides. He said he had loved art since he was a young man in the city and had gotten to know an artist named Charles Sheeler, who was apparently famous but new to me. I now saw Sheeler's surprisingly deep and romantic treatments of industrial scenes. And then I came upon Hoppers like those I had sought in vain at the Met. And after that I was standing in front of Arshile Gorky's portrait of himself as a small child with his mother in Armenia shortly before the mother starved to death in the Turk-led genocide. And then I was looking at an abstract Gorky called *The Betrothal*, which seemed to be about danger and betrayal, and was more literal than abstract to me, and I knew I was getting connected visually again, to the bad and to the good, in ways I had always wanted. As might happen when reading a well-told tale, I was placing myself right in these pictures. Getting information by induction not deduction. And I did not stop looking in museums and galleries for many, many months, and I only paused in the times, starting a year later, that I was myself drawing and painting.

clothed and naked

The phone rang again and again in this new happy, busy, non-writing time, and though I screened I almost always picked up. But I never answered when I heard it was Myra Mindell, former school teacher and not-so-confident editor at this young adult oriented publishing house for which I'd been doing small hack-tinted bread-and-butter books for nearly 20 years. Books with low but steady royalties that sold mainly to school libraries and were easy to do and took up very little of my time. These were sometimes books on countries I'd known well – Indonesia, Jordan – but they were in the catalog side by side with other books on countries written by members of American government or corporate world families that are housed in gated compounds and so know almost nothing of the foreign places they are in. And my next to last little book for this publisher had been one in a bigger format with photographs about modern China.

And, to my horror, not long before I'd begun screening out the school library publisher, that China book had sat for several weeks in an outdoor display window of the Donnell Library – you could not miss it when you crossed 53RD Street from the Museum of Modern Art – and to my shame my name was on it in big letters, the pretentious three-name author name I had used a decade back on the published novel that was supposed to change my life forever – and I had not confessed to the low-advance-paying bread-and-butter publisher that in my last go-round in Asia I still had not gotten into China – and still worse, I wasn't sure it would matter to them that a book on modern China was by someone who had never seen it – who wrote it because he had the contract before he went abroad this last time and because he was in financial trouble and needed the second half of the small advance money.

The phone was still ringing and I was still ignoring Myra Mindell. It was as if those calls were meant in some petty way to pull me back from all the richness of the life I was in. So I had not answered any questions that appeared on my machine about my recent manuscript for that publisher, which was a little historical book about John Cabot and the northern route to the New World, which made me yawn. And I had not answered any of her written questions either, and then I had not responded to Myra Mindell's silly little editorial changes, and after that I had not responded when they had sent me the manuscript after it had gone through a copy editor and was ready for production.

And my sorry, faking-it China book had been in the Donnell Library window when I crossed from the Modern Art Museum.

Though now – months that felt like decades later – there was something parallel going on up on 57TH Street.

As I crossed 57TH Street from near Carnegie Hall I saw in a display case on the façade of the Art Students League's wonderful old French Renaissance building two pastel paintings of mine – two portraits, faces of alive women, actual women I had just drawn and painted from life. Women I had actually seen.

And I had found while drawing and painting them that, as opposed to China, the fact that they had been there right in front of me posing without clothes on was my only hope of getting their faces right.

the last line first

For six mostly happy years I thought I was not a writer.

During this period of not writing the whole landscape of my life, past and present, was changing. I moved from New York City up to Woodstock in the Catskill Mountains, but that was not the whole story. It seemed to me I had lived too much of my life in a linear world involving words. And then words were suddenly useless, and nothing was happening on a straight line.

This change in direction began in the eighties when, while living in Manhattan, I realized I felt less and less connection with what I thought of as my life. Maybe I had had only moderate success with my writing but my identity was as a writer. I had enough money. I had this book my friend Max and I had written on the horror of the Marcos Philippines (one in a string of my mixed-bag published works). The Marcos book was in a bookstore window I passed on Fifth Avenue. A divorce had come through and my social life was picking up. I still had connections to the literary world. I was putting together plans for new books, including one on great rivers of the world and one making fun of California. An editor was pushing a new project that treated my often very dark childhood and family as amusing and happy. There was no satisfaction in any of the projected writing projects that I had thought I wanted so badly. It all felt more like an ending than a beginning, more like death than life.

I was struck with the realization that it had been 20 years since I had written without a contract and advance money. Worse, it had been nearly as long since I had started a book, fiction or nonfiction, without knowing what I would say in my final chapter. Publishers need outlines before they write checks. The outlines are mainly to convince their hard-headed sales people that there will really be a book one day. They are kind of fake, these outlines. But I had been lashed to actual or imagined outlines for years. And nothing was changing. There was no discovery. I began to think of writing as plodding and distant. With new acquaintances I started to hide what I had done for a living.

And now I was spending time alone in museums every day – and was still doing so a year later when I was in art school studio courses all over the city and became, in mid-life, a full-time art student. Now, I thought, as I roamed about town with my portfolio case, no one will take me for a writer.

Operating in visual worlds I found I had no control over what I was doing. It was a relief. I could not use paint and colored pencils to force conclusions and keep terror at bay the way I had taught myself to use words. Maybe an artist with years of academic training could keep up the illusion of control with images the way I had done it with words. But I did not have those years of training. Anything could happen.

I would see something in color – for instance, the horror of blood red against a Flemish or Dutch aqua sky – in the Met; I would be led to that same color combination in an angry East Village feminist crucifixion scene, and that mood would lead to the dark dangerous forests of Hobbema at the Frick, landscapes that I had once thought uneasily should be comforting. Hobbema would lead to the sickly landscapes of Theodore Rousseau at the Frick and the Brooklyn, and then on to the sacred, evocative nature scenes of Daubigny at the Brooklyn and back to the Met again, and then on to visual connections resulting from black between Manet and Goya and Murillo, and then the pure color of Monet at the Met and the Guggenheim and the Modern, the same Monet who had moved me decades earlier in Paris and then been lost to me. And from Monet I would go to Hopper's sunlight on buildings and his wife's grand naked body at the Whitney, then into the horror world of Gorky and the chaos of Pollack, and the lively erotic bronze nudes of Matisse and the strangely evocative but stylized bronze nudes of Archipenko, and the terror of Franz Kline abstract figures, and the deep longing in Joan Mitchell abstractions. Surrealism, I learned, could be as real as realism and abstraction could be too. I did not study art history. I did not know if anyone else saw what I saw. I just looked.

And it was now that the art I saw and made became mixed with images in my dreams, and mixed too with my memories of all the scenes of my life. My stories began to change. For example, episodes of family violence, from suicide to child molestation, no longer seemed isolated incidents in overall stories that I had recounted as amusing. I had found that, though it seemed it could be a great career boosting move, I could not write a word of this projected project in which I planned to treat myself and my family so lightly that all darkness was removed.

Lies no longer seemed unimportant. And maybe this was why for the first time since adolescence I had a sense that spiritual talk was not always nonsense talk. And so I eased into spiritual areas I had dismissed as not fitting my plans – worlds I had dismissed maybe even to the extent that my family of origin had dismissed people of all races including even the race they thought of as their own. (I had once spoken with pride of how I had spent a total of seven intense years in the Far East without having a single spiritual experience.)

Then art led to nature, and I realized how far I had come from forces whose power had once put me in thrall. It is hard to visit the Brooklyn Museum without going to the Brooklyn Botanic Garden, hard to do the Met or the Frick or the Guggenheim without roaming in Central Park. I found myself spending time in nature in a seamless transition from what I had been doing in studio classrooms and in galleries and museums.

I went beyond the parks – to Vermont and New Hampshire, to

New England mountains and lakes. And there seemed no good reason not to live in countryside again. One day I drove up to the Catskills to check out the Woodstock School of Art. I found myself in the surrounding mountains, alongside streams and ponds. As it became clear I would stay I started to know joy and terror I had kept at a distance living in cities for so many years. It had been an array of places, from Bangkok to Beirut to Athens, but always cities, always walking on concrete, not real earth, nothing like the dangerous earth I now remembered – as paintings became mixed with recently salvaged memories, and with dreams, and the present reality.

My stories, now out of my control, took many directions. What I had dismissed as silly I now saw as deadly, and what I had thought of as beyond possibility began to seem real. In this way the landscape of my life, past as well as present, changed. Now nothing was more important than getting at the stories that were most real, which were not always the stories that fit into the imposed frameworks I had accepted.

a surprising appearence

Back when my painting was becoming precise, a time just after late-in-life art school, when I was becoming increasingly sure with light and shade, color and form, perspective and anatomy, back at a time when I had moved to Woodstock in the Catskill Mountains and thought I would never write again – one day back then I began to draw an imaginary but real-seeming lizard-like armored male figure.

Quite real, I thought, for back then, like much of the time now, I feared the overuse of archetypes.

This figure, which I saw in my mind's eye with clarity before I started, would be a compilation of what I hated most. A huge black lizard-like man standing in my way, a lizard in slimy titanium skin and filled with hypocrisy and bigotry, bullying and boorishness, sadism and stupid militarism – a lizard who had suddenly appeared on my most familiar path through the wooded area I loved most in what was now my town.

It had started as a suggested therapeutic writing enterprise – clinical therapy more than art – in which I had selected the villain who would be on the path and written towards my conclusion. A moving exercise in which it felt like something was happening. But it was my old style of writing, the writing I had at this time rejected in favor of drawing and painting. The kind of writing in which you are always moving towards a pre-determined conclusion. This particular conclusion did not stay in place long even in that kind of writing, and in painting there was almost instant transformation.

I knew, as I formed the conception, that some people would have different ideas about such an imaginary chance meeting with some stranger so unlike what they thought of as themselves. Some might think first that such a meeting would really be an encounter with fine or horrible untapped aspects of themselves. Not me. To me it was clear who and what the enemy was – to the sorrow of the linear-minded therapist who had laid out this exercise and was promoting the simplistic idea that any stranger in the imagination had to be nothing more nor less than the client's own self. In other words, you were supposed to write but you were supposed to write only to a predetermined end. How like those light-weight writing classes that tell you to stay in control by writing the last line first.

A few days after seeing the therapist, I dutifully started on a blank 24- by 36-inch canvas to do the threatening armored figure I had seen in my mind. I started with a sable brush sketching with a black fast-drying kind of oil paint thinned with turpentine. I began with confidence, this figure that in my head was so clear. He was enclosed in scaly armor. He was a racist, sadistic bully.

Somehow this black bully figure was supplanted by a quite luscious and mysterious woman. Involuntarily, it seemed, I moved into color, and what seemed to me a huge, strong woman's face and fine bare shoulders appeared in the foreground, and she was surveying a world I did not recall ever having seen.

This world, this landscape stretching out under her mysterious gaze, looked South American to me – maybe the South America that Pizarro and Cortez found – though that was a continent I had never visited.

And I did not know if I hated or liked this woman. And my anger, so carefully directed at greedy, racist, violence-prone right-wingers and other abusers, was becoming something far more complex, far more profound.

In this time when I was not writing.

In this time when there was still so much of my life that I had never begun to write about.

Every once in a while I bring out this painting, look at that full-color, smooth woman with golden skin whom I'd meant to be an armored, slippery, sharp-clawed poison-fanged man. I look at this woman and the mysterious scene that began to unfold beneath her as long forgotten stories, concrete stories, from early in my life fought their way back into the life I was living in the present. This smooth woman, who made the slimy reptilian bully seem tame. This painting and this story that cannot be wrapped up neatly and set aside.

I was busy in this time. New friends. New interests. Travel. Art and nature. A life in art. And in the raw material of theology. And I knew whatever was happening – in this step into mystery – it was only just beginning. Knew it at the moment that the planned lizard became something for which I did not yet have words.

reality of summer days

When I counted them later while taking stock, it would seem like I had had a lot of dates in the museums – from someone I'd known in Beirut to someone I'd just met at the Art Students League, but in context these dates were so rare as to be outside the picture, for I was in the museums more than once a day, for many, many crucial months, and in memory I was almost always alone, seeing art works and my life in challenging and harsh and soft new ways.

I stood in front of one of the Met's Hobbemas while an escorted group came through and they were being told about how every leaf on the trees in Hobbema's 17TH-century forest looked real and brought up a gentle summer day – this scene in very dark woods that I very gradually realized were not at all safe and gentle and summery. I found myself complaining to myself about myself – how could I, a man so attuned to nature, I asked myself, how could I not respond to this moving evocation of a placid summer day in a clearing in gentle summery woods?

Right behind the Hobbema there was a door leading to a high balcony surrounding a bright and airy courtyard, many stories high and lit with real light from a sweeping skylight and a wall of glass that brought in the park from outside. A place with benches to sit on and contemplate in the middle of this airy courtyard what seemed to me light-hearted bits and pieces of popular art – an actual Greek revival bank façade from somewhere in the Middle West, colorful if rather nice-nice works in Tiffany glass, and an amusing carved church pulpit with circular steps and on the top an extremely tight-ass angel heralding some version of something with a trumpet. In this imaginative courtyard, which felt like a holiday place, I felt better. But then I went up on the balcony again and back in that door to old Dutch paintings, and I stood again looking at the summer day woods scenes and I was no closer to being able to enter what I still thought must be the immensely appealing Hobbema world.

That night and sporadically for succeeding nights my dreams took me to those 17TH-century woods in the Dutch lowlands – those woods that in dreams were so very dark, so deadly dangerous, woods in which I became lost – woods that I knew once existed in lowland Holland, but now for me had morphed into the dark high altitude woods of my often dangerous childhood in New Hampshire's White Mountains. That place that in memory, as memory was meant to be in my family, was supposed to be the mold for perfect summer days.

I kept returning to that Hobbema and to another in the Met and one in the Frick. They had something I had to see – something that took me to dark places that lay deep in my heart and mind, so deep down they had nearly been forgotten, and now I was back there – pictures on the wall of museums taking me back. For the darkness and the danger were so clearly present in my past now. And it was so freeing now that I could see it. Matisse's *Piano Lesson* did this for me too – that woman hovering above the imprisoned child at the piano, whose child's glance nonetheless goes to a smooth bronze woman, one of Matisse's own small sculptures playing a role in his painting – the naked bronze girl as warm as the hovering woman is cold.

And then I hunted up the Arshile Gorkys that had deadly sexuality – his non-representational paintings of exposed thorns and razor sharp edges, genital shapes of domination that are a diagram into the necessity for suicide – far more so than his early painting in the Whitney of his mother in Turkish-held Armenia, shown close to when she died of starvation in the genocide time.

Then I was drawing and painting myself, studying around the clock, and I tried to do that black, threatening lizard-like figure of what I thought I would find more threatening than anything else – a scaly, black, lizard-like armor-wearing stranger. And this was when that lizard figure morphed into an enigmatic woman with a sweet but also strong face and luscious bare shoulders, the woman appearing from some strange place as I painted, appearing standing high above a perhaps mythical landscape that I found myself portraying, a landscape I was not aware I had ever seen before, just as I was not aware there was such a smooth bare woman who would appear, standing, so smooth and bare, high above an unending landscape of jagged mountains and deep gorges with zigzagging waters rushing through.

This was when I was not writing because my writing had become so predictable, if saleable, that it was of no use to me and, I knew, would be of no use to anyone else. In my writing in the time when I decided to stop writing, the scaly stranger would have been set in place so there could be no surprises – like something dead.

But then I began to wonder what might happen in writing if I just let what was there appear, let the scenes and the connections come, get out of the way of my art in writing as I was doing in visual realms. I wondered. But meanwhile I had painting.

I had turned my one-bedroom apartment, which had a southern view over rooftops almost to the Battery, into a studio. I built wide, heavy shelves for art materials, everything removed from the walls except my drawings and paintings, my perspective studies and my color wheels, my anatomical diagrams and soft flesh pastels, the bed removed to leave space for easels and armatures and plaster casts of humans or their bones or muscles, and a drafting table.

I would wake up at dawn on a daybed and know what was around me. But also know how the landscape of my life had changed. How seemingly safe people in my personal landscapes past and present and future had been revealed as betrayers, even molesters. How neo-Victorian family members – intelligent, sometimes honored, cautiously Ivy League – family members who had seemed at worst comic in their stuffiness had turned into people who now seemed like characters in horror stories. Despite their veneer, they had left in their wake molestation and addiction and hopeless depression, and the often violent early deaths of sons and daughters. Like Cousin Elka who had just killed herself. Like Cousin Margaret who, apparently cured of cancer, said she wanted to die and did die. Like Cousin Deirdre, far from dead but beaten and fucked from the time she was seven till the time she was sixteen, when the brother who did it to her was killed in a mysterious accident.

In the early morning I would lie on the day bed for a time in a suspended state, as if there had just been a major death and as if, if I kept my eyes closed, I could pretend it had not happened yet. These many cousins from summer days in White Pines who had become the dead or the walking dead.

Lying on the daybed in what was now my crowded studio, my eyes shut, remembering, then, paintings visited and revisited for the hope they gave me. Matisse's harsh but still connected piano lesson – Deibenkorn's capturing of life-giving color, Joan Mitchell's exuberance, Manet's reality, and Daubigny, among the painters new to me – his use of green in river bank scenes causing me to breathe deeply with happiness, and remember something wonderful this time that I knew once and had nearly forgotten, and had not, in my professional writing life, had words for. Knowing now that this was what I wanted, both the light and the blackness. This I should write about, and to get to the light I had to go through those woods again.

the awful romans

In that time when everything was changing and even before I had started to draw, a wide lampshade in my apartment was lined with scores of those different colored Metropolitan Museum buttons that proved you had paid something to be allowed into the Met on a given day (my payment never close to what the dishonest signs implied was a big required entrance fee, but which in fact was only a donation – a donation of any amount, mine rarely being as low as a penny and never more than a quarter, for I suddenly needed the Met every day). I needed the Met and the Brooklyn and the Guggenheim and the Whitney and the Frick and the Drawing Center and an infinite number of galleries – the places where even before I picked up a pen or brush, I was experiencing these unfoldings in my life for which words had not yet come. Those unfoldings that never would have taken place if I had stayed with linear ways of writing – with silly A to B to C nonsense that "the men of measured merriment" promote.

For many months I hardly noticed the Roman room, which at that time you had to pass through on your way down a corridor lined with strange ancient Cypriot statues of helmeted people with blank eyes. I would move off to the rooms on the right and on the left where the classic Greek statues were placed, grand and perfect in an archetypal way. The classic period Greek statues, of men only, never reminded me of anyone I had known in life, though some later Greek statues, those labeled Hellenistic rather than classic, could be of very real animals or old men and women, or beautiful young women. This so-called degenerate Hellenistic period where actual people could be seen in the art – not just those archetypal statue people. And there was a grave-site relief stone carving of a bigger-than-life young, touching, surely once nurturing woman, her body lightly draped but so soft and lovely even though the stone nose was missing, looking out with a sad expression on her face – a farewell scene, the plaque said, one of the few curator-written plaques in the Met that actually seemed to have something cogent to do with the pictures or statues they claimed to be describing.

Then on each day I would transition from the Greeks to coffee in a big cool cafeteria, in its last days, that looked like something that came from Alexandria or Atlantis – it had a fountain in the recessed center – and after coffee I would move perhaps too quickly through Oceania and New Guinea to the newly opened 20th-century wing that was annoying the critics because it had art that was not yet, to them, in the canon – and this included now the wonderful Hopper, the mundane Hockney, and the thought-to-be-too-common Curry and Kent, and virtual unknowns, including an artist named Walkowitz who had a painting that was a wild swirl of cities and mountains and a society-looking girl from an earlier time – a scene that an artist who knew some of my stories alerted me to for she found it a portrait of my life.

I would go to the 19th century, and then often follow a passage lined with drawings and photographs, then a detour to a romantic Renaissance courtyard with Bernini figures and sexy Rococo girls and a silly nude Bacchus playing his violin – and then back up the big staircase to the European paintings, which now seemed profoundly like what home could be, if home could be with Rembrandt and Bellini. And after that maybe over to the strange and grand light-hearted courtyard with that bank building façade and a trumpeting angel and a bronze Diana shooting an arrow, along with the colorful but near stultifying good-taste Tiffany things – and on to the American wing, and the wonderful Winslow Homer and the mundane patriotic muralists, and pornography from early America (a sweet, naked marble white girl captive with her wrists bound just before a raping at the hands of fearsome Indians). And then back to the art that went deep.

And for months going to the Met nearly every day, often twice a day, I did not see the Roman busts as I went through the Roman room. It should have been impossible to miss since you had to go through it to get to the Greeks or to have coffee.

Those portraits of emperors and other prominent Romans – intelligent faces without pity, faces full of cheap, clever irony without any understanding.

And then one day I stopped and saw where I was, and knew, though the curator plaques implied the opposite, that the Romans had no art unless you counted these mug-shot portrait busts, these very precise renderings of emperors and their wives and relatives and hangers-on the way they wanted to be depicted – otherwise no art except grandiose buildings for cruel administrators – no art except copies of the works of their betters, the Greeks – but nothing else except these mug-shot busts ordered up by the very people who gloried in their cruelty – these cold busts of clever, heartless people whose appeal I knew too well.

It was the sort of recognition I had felt years back when Joe Abbey read the story told by Browning's cold, cruel duke – or when in Shakespeare I encountered the malevolent cliché-spouting Polonius.

And it seemed to me, though I was doing my best now to avoid fixed ideas, that right now these Roman figures had far more weight than the idealized figures of the Greeks. The archetypal Greek figures seemed for detached intellectual admiration. But these recreations of real Romans stirred up real memories and feelings.

That day when I paused in the Roman room I heard myself expressing gratitude that that ancient world had died. That world that produced those faces, the world that was proud of those faces – thank God, although I did not then believe in any god – "Thank God," I heard myself saying aloud, while all these cruel emperors and hangers-on and consorts, including some who could have been my closest associates, looked out from a distant past which could have been the recent past – they looked out from antiquity and turned their stares on me.

Those Romans who had almost no art, did horrible things to each other, and did their duty to maintain peace by killing all who disagreed with them. I did not think of myself as Christian then, but "Thank God," I said aloud, "that Christianity came along when it did."

writing as duty

By the time I got out of the army, 24 years old, I felt I had really made a start in living, which to me was the same thing as thinking I had made the right moves to be a writer. It was to be a life that went far beyond the exhortation to think only of duty.

For nine months I had been a wire service journalist. I had flown out to Indianapolis, at 21, the day after graduation from college, to join the old United Press, for which I was immediately covering politics, which in Indiana meant very extreme right-wing politics, a situation that began to fall into place when I realized that nearly everyone whom I was following – the governor, both senators, most of the legislative leaders – had been around since the thirties, when the Klan ran the state and you could no more embark on a political career without the Klan in Indiana than you could have a career in government in Germany if you were not with the Nazis.

Writing news stories was fascinating, putting all these things into words that would pass my bureau chief, who had always been in Indiana. I had to figure how to get in my contempt for what was happening and still give the appearance of objectivity. Being a strict grammarian, he gave me some outs. When I was writing about anti-labor legislation, which went hand-in-glove with everything else the four-to-one Republican legislature was passing – such as expanding the death penalty so that it could be used on juveniles who commit nighttime burglary – I could get away with saying a bill just signed by the governor was for a new "so-called" right-to-work law. This union-busting bill. "So-called." I may have gotten away with it for to get a real feel for the adjective "so-called" you have to hear it said with a Brooklyn or Bronx accent. My editor, Boyd Gill (men I met in Indiana tended to be named Boyd), who was so a part of the place that his lapel pin identified him as a past president of Kiwanis, said "so-called" was okay because it just meant that something was called something.

From Indiana I, now 22 years old, went straight to Cuba, looking for Castro and his Robin Hood-like band. I was in and out of a Batista army jail on the edge of the Sierra Maestra, and then in and out of tiny fishing boats that went out of sight of land in the hunt for fish bigger than the boats, and in and out of brothels that put in the shade even the whorehouses in Indianapolis when the legislature was in session. Then I was in Atlanta, nominally in the draft-filled peacetime army but also working full time for United Press again. And on the edge of history, it seemed, here at the start of the civil rights movement.

I summarized my first years. A Klan-run state, a foreign revolution, the civil rights movement – the sort of thing that should go on a young author's dust jacket. And, moreover, a searing affair with a married woman, and to top it off, a non-paying affair with a call girl. How like a legendary writer.

And I almost started a magazine that had the immodest goal of supplanting the tired old *New Yorker*. And then I was living in New York on the Lower East Side, still a good deal of drama, and back to wire service journalism again. And for the first time since I had decided firmly not to go to law school I asked myself if this was really what I wanted. And then I got this idea that I could be like the man in that recent movie *The Blackboard Jungle*. I could go teach in some inner New York City school – for I knew the crucial racial matters that were in the air in this time, not just in the south but up here too. I would get into the middle of it as a real person, not as a bystander reporter.

No one thought this was a good idea. My former college roommate, who had been an outspoken near-Socialist, was in the city starting as an associate with an old-line Wall Street law firm, Cravath, Swain & Moore, working on corporate tax matters. He said that under no circumstance should I throw my life away like this.

That reaction surprised me. Even Jim saying to play it safe. And then years later there was something similar. I had abandoned projects for which I had been paid advances, two books that were meant to be big books, and I, 44 now, was in a marriage with a girl I thought would be so different from what I came from, not only a non-Wasp but a non-American, a non-white person, a non-alcoholic – and then I had that trite experience I had heard so much about and thought this could never happen to me. I woke up beside her one morning and realized she was, for my life now, what my mother had been long ago under dark clouds in Connecticut.

And I thought for the first time in 20 years that now I must really make a break with what fate planned for me. I didn't like what I was writing. I didn't like my life. I just could not finish what I was writing. I didn't like what I had become.

And now the old inner school teaching idea came up again. And all my old friends in the city – Walter, who was becoming a celebrated political writer, Alex, the very successful author of wine books, John, who now climbed major mountains – they seemed to recoil in horror, just like my old college roommate long ago. Alex and John were on the same page with Walter, who said firmly that "writers are supposed to write."

writing of a sort

I realized later that during that time I was away from writing I never stopped all versions of writing. I carried notebooks with me when I was in museums or roaming in city and country places I had known in the past, or new places, like Arezzo and Urbino, that I had never seen before and that I was absorbing visually. Or when I was in groups in which people were searching for what had happened in the past. I would have an idea and I would jot it down. And it would stay there in my notebook just the way I had conceived it in my head.

And so even though I was filling up notebooks with thoughts, writing was still not very useful to me. It did not, like painting now, turn my life upside down – my life, which is the only life I know well enough to place at the center of my art.

By writing down insights and reminders to myself I was not writing in the sense of recreating reality. I was journaling – which has become a popular pastime and can be important, for it entails recording things the author knows and making declarations about them. But the main reader of a writer's journals is the writer's own self, and so it is not necessary to do the full scenes and stories that are already in the writer's head.

Sometimes journaling yields important results, for it can give an accurate picture of what is happening in the head, and it can be a way to lay out the pros and cons of decisions that face the writer. It can also be useful for future writing, for it is a start at laying out the writer's raw material. But journaling – unless faked for a course requirement – still means writing for the writer's own self only, and with no need to recreate scenes. For some teachers, required journaling is a way for the student to get thoughts in order and pull together what the student is learning from life and from reading. For some other teachers, it is something far from admirable. Some rigid academics, who glorify linear thinking, despise the intuitive and personal and never take chances, still put a journaling requirement in their courses. They consider it that safe.

It is in the process of recreating reality that an artist strikes gold. In the process of going from head to canvas or paper a fixed idea in the head is transformed into something much more. And this always means bringing scenes to life so that even a stranger can see what is there. It is in this process of creation and recreation that challenging changes so often appear. And it is worth remembering all art is directed towards some sort of audience – in the new present or the far future – directed towards people who will eventually see your painting, people who will hear your music, people who, way down the line perhaps, will read your books – and perhaps will read them right away if your chapters go up on line. You are creating something that is crucial to you and hence is sure to mean something to others. To be clear to the viewer or listener or reader you cannot just refer to things. It is that old but true line that you must show, not just tell. In journaling you do not need to show. You do not need recreate anything. You merely refer to matters which are already clear in your head. And so you do not get into the process of creation. And you are likely to suffer from the limits of logic.

A few years into my non-writing time I went to a weekend "inner child" retreat in which we were all told to "write a letter to yourself as a child." I wasn't writing anymore, I thought, but I went walking by a river and I wrote this letter to myself with some emotion and great sympathy, wondering where I had been all these years. And when I read this piece I choked up. But something was lacking. At the end of what I wrote I was precisely where I had been when I started. There had not been discovery, just a reiteration of matters already known – though what it did tell me, and where it had been useful, was that I was not finished with my childhood yet.

I read the piece aloud and the retreat leader/therapist gave a wise look and said, "You are writing again, Fred." And later he was still taking credit for my return to writing. But I knew at the retreat that this was not real writing yet. I think it was important to him that he had a published writer as a client.

That letter-to-a-child thing. It only goes so far – this kind of therapy writing. For it is usually carefully directed, sometimes quite subtly, by the one who gives the assignment. It starts with a conclusion. This does not always happen, but it is very likely to happen in therapy writing, which is so much like journaling. It is worth repeating that here in journaling you are dealing with the same raw material that goes into the best of writing, the best of art. But the therapy version of journaling rarely leads into mystery in the way art can. Cézanne spoke of art as being creation that is taking place simultaneously, and in much the same way, as divine creation. Writers come to know that an idea in the head – where logic prevails – invariably becomes something else when it is put to the test on paper – when the writer goes into actual scenes and stories and brings them to life.

And then there was the dark scaly stranger. He had appeared in another therapy exercise. The idea was to write about an imaginary encounter with some fearsome stranger who has always been around. So I made the stranger this one-dimensional, slimy, scaly, bullying bigot. How very satisfying.

It was a few weeks later, when alone in my studio, that I tried a visual response. This was when I started that painting that was supposed to be of this bigoted stranger who had haunted me all my life. A stranger so simple as to be easily put down. But when I painted him I could not keep him so simple that I could dismiss him and never miss him. I could not keep this stranger in such a safe place. A much more formidable person appeared in the place of the scaly man – this woman with glorious, golden skin who was looking down on a mysterious, exotic, lovely and craggy landscape – a landscape which to enter would mean entering the unknown.

In the retreat leader/therapist's simplistic world it would have been, and was, said that in the exercise you would find the stranger to be yourself. But I was not that woman, although if she were not important to me, were not part of me, she would not have appeared in my art. What I was finding was too complicated for smug psychological dictums. Complicated in the mind when clear in the heart.

All painting at this point was exciting to me. What I did not know quite yet was that writing could be too – which was what I had thought about writing in the first place before the years of living by writing.

the end of insight

Words. Faith in words. I think of the saints, all of whom wrestle with faith in ways that mere pious people never do. I was no saint, in either life or literature, but I had wrestled with faith in words the way correct, orthodox writers never do. And I had fled writing for six years, like a monk fleeing a monastery.

I had lived on writing for 30 years and then come to despise writing, which came to seem as false and useless to me as would a failed religion. When I did come back to the written word after six years away there were certain things I did not anticipate – as in making the mistake of thinking I could also come back to my old faith in the logic of outcomes, logic being so tied to the use of words. I was back as if my return had been inevitable, my sudden need now for words as well as images to find out what had happened and who I was. And now I had to figure out what this return to words would mean in a life that had been so satisfying without words.

The changes that had come in my life in this period when I was not writing had led to many surprises, not the least being conscious awareness for the first time of spiritual hunger for realms where I did not have the illusion I could know outcomes before I stepped into them – real life being like real writing in which so much happens that I would be a fool, I now thought, to start with a fixed, untested if logical conclusion and think I could live my way into it.

My world had changed so much that at the time when I was returning to writing I was studying at a university – something I would not have gone near in my professional writing years and was very careful about now. But I did not go to study writing. I went to look into theology.

The university was this marvelously open and liberal Jesuit place, Boston College – part of a Catholic world that I had often respected when seen as an agnostic, and that I had been careful to avoid intellectually, though its intellectuals attracted me.

What really attracted me most, over the years when I was outside it, was its warmth and daring. I had missed warmth and daring in a self-consciously respectable Episcopalian family – though in adolescence I did have a loving Catholic girlfriend. Most of what I knew of Catholic worlds at first hand came later and had nothing to do with harsh nuns wielding rulers or silly anti-Communists or people who picketed worthy movies, but rather with people I encountered in dangerous places who did not fit the anti-Catholic clichés – especially quietly heroic clerical and lay activists in places like Taiwan and the Borneo part of Indonesia, and Somoza's Nicaragua and the Haiti of the Duvaliers and the Philippines of the Marcoses.

And right now, as part of what I was doing at Boston College, I was across the Charles River at a place called Weston exploring the 16TH-century Spiritual Exercises of Ignatius of Loyola – and it meant writing again. For the exercises entail stepping right into stories, which might be stories from the past but will inevitably be the writer's most crucial stories in the present. People I knew now had used the exercises to change their lives – to leave religious life or go into it – to leave or go into marriages – to leave or to take on careers and vocations – and I was captivated by the Ignatian proposition that you could find God's will if you stepped into your story this way. It was not that I thought there was no revelation outside the Catholic church. And not that I had a liking for the right-wing Pope. But I went now for Ignatian spirituality. And I went now for the reassuring view of James Joyce whose definition of Catholicism, as reiterated by my mentor Tom Groome, was "Here comes everyone."

Yet in conflict with what I was discovering, I made a serious error in my return now to writing. I thought that with words I could and should bring logic back into my life again. Some saints, after all, had spoken of logic as one of God's gifts. And so I wrote with intense rationality to figure out something that concerned me night and day at this moment I was studying Ignatius.

I was on the verge of making a major move in my life – another marriage, this time to a bright and sexy woman with two children. The connection I was about to make meant I would have to come to terms with how one of the children, a coddled, sarcastic boy, lorded it over everyone as the designated prince in his family – the one who got the good grades and always managed to please his elders – which to me meant an insufferable good-boy, this potential stepson. This boy who took short cuts to please his elders, and spent energy on putting down his vibrant younger sister. It was so disturbing, the prospect of living with this guy, that I thought maybe I better drop the marriage, even though I wanted it. I was keyed up and horny and did not want to back out. And maybe was overreacting. So I decided I would write about the situation as honestly as I could, and see where I came out.

And I got a good part of the story right, including that the adventurous younger sister seemed to have the real potential in fields that were supposed to be her older brother's alone – writing and drawing included. And that this was forbidden to anyone else in the family except her brother. Some members seemed to delight in predicting a horrible end for this engaging girl, who was just now entering her teens. The boy was skilled at putting his sister down and was not above lies and some larceny and at the same time, in the family version, he was still the good little boy – the good little boy even though his actual age was 20.

And as I wrote about all this – *about* it more than *in* it – I began to see an overriding reason why the situation was so upsetting to me that it felt like unmanageable chaos even though I wanted the marriage. This son was a family policeman enforcing a false family version of reality. He was billed as the artistic one, but he was also, it seemed to me, the one stopping art and life from breaking out. It seemed to me as I wrote that he had exactly the role in his family and with his sister that my twin brother, Peter, had had in our family and with me. (Years after we had left home, my parents acquired two gray cats who were brothers and named them Good Cat and Bad Cat.)

Both Peter and this boy, I thought, had been forced into what they did for the benefit not of themselves but of their families. Fulfilling sick needs of others. But although I could feel, or at least thought I should feel, compassion for them as victims, these were situations dominated by the most harmful sorts of false versions of reality.

And then I made the mistake of thinking that this insight, tying the boy to my brother and to ideas about false and also alternative versions of reality, was enough. I was thinking again, as I had before big changes in my life began, that insight ever could be enough. And so again I used insight to go against something I knew. If I could get to the correct formulation of what I faced, I could handle it all, I thought. And so I did what I had wanted to do in the first place. I went ahead with the marriage. And I really did want this woman.

And the marriage started to fall apart at the start, and despite energy and money and insight, and some inadequate couples therapy, it very soon fell apart altogether. And I very soon knew I never would have gotten into it if I had really stepped into the story when I wrote about it, which was probably what Ignatius meant – recreated the story so that it was in my bones, as opposed to burying it in insight.

the *how* to write industry

I suspected the marriage did not stand much of a chance when my then wife thought it was great that my stepson was so pleased with his poetry writing class, which was centered around keeping control of your work by always writing the last line first, then filling in whatever needs to be filled in so that you can get to that last line and nowhere else.

But I can understand the appeal, for if the ending is there before you begin you can pretty well dispense with anything precarious that might appear while in the writing process. In effect, you have thrown out process. If you already have the ending in place, then nothing very bad can happen. And nothing will ever change.

There is a vast industry that tends to silence real artists and that I believe is based on fear. I call it the How-to-Write Industry. It is something like what Leonard Bernstein called "the music appreciation racket." Non-artists take over, promote criticism above creativity, and set up rules and limits to what artists can or should do. And thus art, including the art of writing, becomes something so safe it threatens no fossilized ideas.

The How-to-Write industry can make itself felt in academic writing programs, starting with English 101, where silly rules often come in and the silliness of such things as learning rhetorical modes. Its rules are often felt in back-biting M.F.A. programs in creative writing, almost all of the commercial writing workshops and the huge number of on-line writing courses a web search turns up, as well as in writing magazines for the public and little writing journals for the academics. In all these areas there are sympathetic, empathetic teachers that one would be fortunate to encounter. But there are many more teachers who exalt criticism at the expense of art and do not welcome real stories. In many of these courses, as in a majority of books about writing, it is as if nothing is real, everything is an exercise or a system for writing-to-order. And writing is meant to be such an ordeal that there are programs that use the word "boot camp" in their titles or promotional materials.

But though writing can be hard, the pure-ordeal notion cannot be taken seriously by a writer who is actually writing from what that writer knows, sees, feels and finds inside herself or himself. In fact, in the Authentic Writing workshops and in our one-on-one sessions it often seems that the very best writing comes in ways that feel natural and even easy. It is the falsification involved in the writing-to-order kind of writing – in writing meant to fit someone else's version of reality – that causes anguish and blockage – like a time during dark days when I tried to turn a searing family story into a happy story for a book editor, or when under contract I tried to write about State Department people as if I admired them – myself then like all those people who will not admit that what they are trying to write has nothing to do with what they believe or who they are or what has really happened.

The How-to-Write Industry keeps coming up with new techniques to stop writing from going anywhere unexpected, anywhere that would cause anxiety to those in power. This industry is like a religion that finds death more appealing than life.

As in a cult, there are How-to-Write laws rooted in dubious scholarship such as the rules, based on Latin, not English, to never start a sentence with a conjunction, never split an infinitive, never end a sentence with a preposition. These rules are calls to stop doing things that all the best writers constantly do when they allow the writing itself to take over. And there are other rules constantly violated in major literature that, if followed to the letter, are just as bad – such as "Avoid the passive voice" or "Adhere strictly to your outline." These are things that at best might be somewhat helpful as fixed rules if your only ambition were to write catalog blurbs or small appliance assembly instructions.

One thing my brother did, trying to be helpful as I was returning to writing, was sign me up in the Writer's Digest Book Club. And just then the Writer's Digest magazine's special memoir issue came out. It was filled with advice for writing memoir. Write only about people you have known, it said, really interesting people. Don't write about yourself.

Much in the manner of those prissy grade school teachers who ban the use of "I" – for who would be interested in such as you?

I heard a good many horror stories when I did a two-day writing workshop for a group of high school age, college-aspiring, often undocumented daughters and sons of migrant and other unprotected farm and orchard workers. Although memoir writers commonly do not get going until their middle years, there are exceptions – like one of the members of this migrant and farm-worker group.

Natasha was a vibrant young woman of color who was clearly too smart for high school. She had been writing fine poetry and prose on her own, she said, but she now was in a high school English class in New York State's depressed Orange County in which the fair-skinned teacher had been throwing out all sorts of horrible new rules, framed by an absolute ban on Natasha's using the first person.

The teacher sometimes gave her students a Xeroxed paragraph that they were to use as the opening paragraph of their own essays. Then she went into more strictures that were new even to me, a collector of horrible writing rules. She told her students that in every paragraph the last sentence must always repeat everything said in the first sentence, and warned that anyone would be flunked who wrote a paragraph containing more than one thought.

Natasha said she asked the teacher why she had to follow these rules. The teacher replied with what I think is an unintentionally fitting motto for the How-to-Write Industry. "You must follow these rules," the teacher said, "because this is the white people's way of writing."

without *embalming* fluid

I was like someone who has sojourned far from a familiar place, and when that person returns he finds there have been earthquakes and forest fires and hurricanes, and although the place has been quickly and carefully rebuilt to cover up the damage, nothing remains the same.

As I was coming into my story it was not just my version of the family I came from that changed. For example, I was a person who stayed clear of academic worlds. For further example, for years my profile in *Twentieth Century Authors* had me down as atheist/agnostic.

I went to Boston College to take a three-week intensive summer course that intrigued me. It was given by David Tracy, a liberal American theologian and priest widely celebrated in theological circles and beyond. His picture had recently been on the cover of the *New York Times Sunday Magazine.*

I did not know the terminology of theological studies and I was often lost in the specifics of his lectures. Although I had been doing a lot of reading, theology was new to me, and these lectures were full of terms – such as "hermeneutical" – that at that point meant nothing to me. What came across, however, was David Tracy's pastoral presence, a truly good and empathetic man, who had not let logic overwhelm his pastoral bent. He was more interested in life than logic. And so too were the others in the big class, who were of all ages and many backgrounds and not at all what I would have expected in either academia or a religious place.

At the end of the Tracy course there was a paper due on the subject of "God Talk." I did not know where to start. And anyway I was no longer a writer. Others spoke of doing such subjects as "God talk in narrative" or "God talk in the synoptic gospels." Well, there was no reason why I had to write if I had nothing to say. This experience so far had been like day to the night of my college years, when having nothing to say would never have gotten in the way of writing nonsense that echoed a professor's bias.

I was enjoying myself and I was game. I drove up to New Hampshire to take a look around the scenes of my deep past. What came up was devastating. I came back. I sat down to write. I had a portable typewriter with me for I had been absent when computers finally took over – that was how remote from writing I had become.

I sat down, wondering what to write, and then suddenly I was in the Roman room at the Metropolitan. And I had my subject – visual God talk.

I had been affected so deeply by that visual experience in the Met, that visual demonstration of a people who had come to a dead end, that I was now immersed in theology – something I had never thought about before in any way except to dismiss it. It is true that shortly before going to Boston I had been talking about the time in the Roman room. But I had never brought the experience to light in the way I did in this supposed academic paper that had become a piece of memoir. I was there in that room I had managed to pass through without seeing, there looking at those faces staring out of a cruel ancient world that were as familiar to me as the faces of all the people I knew and, worse, all the people I had wanted to know.

Not having been raised in a Catholic place or by Catholic people, I had missed a lot but I had been spared exposure to strains in Catholicism that entailed memorization of simplistic catechism answers, right-wing priests and sexual guilt. I had never met a nun who wielded her ruler like an instrument of torture. I now knew beautiful nuns, artistic nuns, freedom fighter nuns, nuns you might not know were nuns. The Catholic world I had entered recently at a Hudson Valley retreat center, and now in Boston, was a world of new openings. And I realized now that in my travels, literal and psychic, I had been getting glimpses for many years of such openings.

The paper that I wrote – which I called "Visual God Talk" – was circulated at Boston College, with a note that it came out of an advanced theology course that by mistake this neophyte had joined. It was about my recent spiritual experiences in art, starting with my experience in the Met's grim Roman room where I suddenly saw how awful the world would have been if Christianity had not come along. The theologian Thomas H. Groome, who was a celebrity in theological circles and would soon be a major mentor and companion to me, was shown the paper and immediately asked to see me.

It had been a long time since I had had a mentor. There had been Joe Abbey my boarding school English teacher. In my Southeast Asia years there had been a close relationship with a Welsh-Englishman Jack Jones, an entertaining and compassionate storyteller whose life had been high adventure and who was the author of *A Woman of Bangkok*, a book that never goes out of print. But this too was long ago.

I accepted an invitation to stay on for a time at Boston College, my lack of academic qualifications notwithstanding, and I let what had started with what was meant to be an academic paper continue – letting my life unfold now on the page.

And then in one of Tom's classes he said that poetry would be as acceptable as a formal academic reflection or research paper. What I once would have thought of as the least likely of all places to do real writing – a university – turned out then to be just right.

Here, unlike in college but very much like in art school, I checked out many courses before I signed up for any of them. And here, as in art school, I was surrounded by faces that were the opposite of what I had seen in cold Roman portrait sculpture – or for that matter what I had seen way back at Princeton.

I did not come here to place myself in the tradition of famous authors, from Graham Greene to Walker Percy who had converted to Catholicism, though I found myself in that tradition. And I did not think that this was the only source of revelation. It was the source I found most congenial. I was, thankfully, operating without a master plan. And I suspected that eventually when I wrote again there would be no more outlines to get in the way of whatever might unfold from mystery.

letting the *stories* come and go

My non-writing time was at an end but I did not know it for sure until I began to work with Tom Groome, this wonderful Irish raconteur and theologian who is the world's leading theorist and practitioner of religious education. He does it in the context of amazing wit and spirituality and caring and natural poetry. I met him in a part of Boston College, its Institute of Religious Education and Pastoral Ministry, that was not a place to get a doctorate in English or an MFA in writing. It was far too creative for that.

I had found myself drawn to Boston and theology in the time I was living outside verbal realms. I was not finished with the art schools, but now there was something else that was just as surprising and just as powerful and seemed all of a piece with this opening into mystery that was opening up my life.

So here I was at an actual academic institution – something I never would have gone near if I had managed, as I did too often in my writing years, to keep ideas in the head frozen by keeping them away from intuition and emotion and the unfolding of mystery. Those days when I could take a chunk of remembered reality and pump it full of intellectual embalming fluid in proper literary fashion so as to keep these thoughts in my head looking like life. I may have been right in the first place about the limits of academia. But this was different.

Tom became my spiritual director and also my academic adviser. I took all his courses, as well as an independent study course we created that allowed me to get credit for writing stories in the guise of researching the effect of literature on theology. And I took him up on his suggestion that maybe for me a pure academic paper was not the thing. And so now I was really writing about my life.

And almost immediately I was 15 years old, not 56, and I was in New Hampshire, happily lost on the page to an even greater extent than I had been happily lost on canvas.

I was in New Hampshire, where one day from a makeshift diving board by a sluice way I, in swimming trunks but wearing a canvas fedora, saw, across the pond, the Grout sisters, who had just come from the train with a cousin visiting for the first time – a smooth dark-haired girl with a heart-warming face, slim but rounded and skin tanned the color of maple sugar. And now I saw across the pond from the diving board that the girls were walking into the water – a scene I knew I would never forget. She was laughing. She was splashing.

I was so excited I dove in, showing off, plunged in with my canvas hat on, and I swam underwater, and I came up, with my hat still on, beside this amazing new girl – Kitty.

And then there was another scene that had almost been over-ridden, almost drowned in constructed forgetfulness. It was a weekday afternoon at White Pines and the place was as empty as death. Through French doors at the living room end of the 80-foot main room I could see bird baths and flowers, but there were no people in the view – which stretched across iron-streaked rocks, and blueberry and thorn fields, out to woods owned by my grandparents – leading to the high mountains, which rose so sharply they seemed to cut off the sun.

Inside, no one is ever around in mid-afternoon – except today. I am here. And Kitty is here. This girl named Kitty who I'd met while I was showing off at a swimming place.

Now at this end of the long room at White Pines I have my blue leatherette portable dorm room record player – still called a Victrola in this house where there is no other record player of any kind. Kitty has brought LPs. Twenties songs. The twenties revival in the fifties. Boop boop a doop. And the Charleston. Everyone she knows at home (where she is about to go into 10TH grade at Greenwich Country Day), everyone is doing the Charleston, she says. The twenties are back. And she'll teach me.

And there I am now, flicking my feet out, operating with hands on knees like Ray Bolger in the movies, as if my legs are rubber and also can cross through each other. We are doing the Charleston.

Peter, my twin, strides through the room. "I see," he says, "Miss Kitty's Dancing Class. Heh heh."

But we keep going! Although I cannot really believe that White Pines is a place for such music.

Maybe not. Or maybe it is.

The Charleston, the Charleston. There'll be a back number when the Charleston, the new Charleston, down in South Caroline.... The Charleston... the Charleston....

So there I was, the past still alive, with Kitty again. But so many of the stories that appeared were hardly Kitty stories. These other stories that had once seemed safe now became horror stories when I got them out of my head and onto paper. Context was being filled in now, and the stories were changing.

Often now parts that had stayed safely in the head led, when written, into dark and dangerous territory. But also, it turned out, nonwritten stories in my head could leave out the most warm and life-giving versions, as in some Kitty times, of what was in the landscape of my life.

Either way, frozen stories are dangerous.

the *definition* of sin

Tom Groome and I had been talking about the past coming in to haunt the present, about how perhaps family members were trying to bring a halt to whatever was opening up. Tom's reaction: "As we say in Ireland, fuck the begrudgers. Let's have a party."

When Authentic Writing began, this was the organization motto. Fuck the begrudgers.

And Tom helped open up to me the late theologian Karl Rahner, who was in and out with the Vatican but fortunately in at the time Pope John XXIII arose, that brief time when everything seemed possible in the Catholic Church.

One night as I sat reading, something happened that was the equivalent of seeing sunshine after years of living in underground caverns. I read a definition of sin:

"That which is not authentic."

I encountered the creative Old Testament scholar Walter Brueggemann, who came to Boston College sometimes in the summers. I heard him give his take on the Exodus story. This story that is known to everyone in the Western world and has guided liberation movements right up through the American civil rights movement, is perhaps the leading guiding story of the Western world – coming from the illogical Israelites from the East who saw the heart as a human's vital center – so different from the Greeks, who academics like to claim are our guides – though I have never encountered anyone who claimed to be guided by a Zeus or an Athena, with the exception of some very bad amateur-night poets.

It became clear to me that artists must shake off the residue left by Plato, who was all for abolishing any art that was not useful propaganda to shore up the power of the Athens slave-state. The philosophical Greeks could be as bad as the militarist Romans. For the Greeks, logic, rather than the affections, rather than intuition and unfolding, was meant to dominate – and their philosophers might well be pleased by what passes for art, the cornball song "God bless America" at the very time the American government is starting wars of choice, breaking treaties, introducing torture as state policy.

In the Brueggemann interpretation, the Israelites were slaves like most people in the ancient world, but something happened in ancient Egypt that set them apart from other slaves. They came to see that the narrative under which they were living, the version of reality that they had accepted, was no more than clever theater designed to propagate the power of the rulers. In other words, they came up with an alternative version of reality in which each human being was honored, and when they did this, all hell broke loose in their land of exile, and before long the Egyptians were begging and bribing them to leave – all except the top Egyptian, the Pharaoh, who tried without success to chase them down and kill them.

An alternative version of reality, Brueggemann pointed out, is automatically, inevitably, subversive and countercultural. All change and progress comes from alternative versions.

Dictators are quite right when they imprison or exile or kill the most creative people in their realms, for nothing is so dangerous to them as a true-self version of reality that goes against a false but triumphal version. A triumphal version may mean a leader sending out death squads. It may mean a perverse family dictator being willing to kill – as tabloid readers know they often are – to preserve a version of reality that places them, even those who molest their children, at the top of their cult-like families.

Then and now, a writer's own true version of reality is always subversive and countercultural to some triumphal version of some very powerful national or family dictator. Dictators who have no trouble with logic, but are deathly afraid of art.

Arts Anonymous

There is a program that used to be called Arts Anonymous. That was not its full name, but it was offered under the 12-step umbrella and that was what people were calling it. In 1987 I went to one meeting of an Arts Anonymous group on St. Mark's Place at the request of a friend of mine who wanted company.

By now there was a burgeoning number of different 12-step programs meeting in Manhattan – not just AA and Alanon and Narcotics Anonymous and Overeaters Anonymous and Gamblers Anonymous and Debtors Anonymous but also Messy Apartments Anonymous, and Latecomers and Procrastinators Anonymous and Co-Dependents Anonymous and Sex Addicts Anonymous (not to be confused with Sex and Love Addicts Anonymous).

This one, however, seemed like a parody of all the rest. The participants in Arts Anonymous introduced themselves as if they were confessing a dangerous addiction. Instead of saying, "My name is so-and-so and I'm an alcoholic," or "My name is so-and-so and I'm a compulsive overeater," in this new program the introductory line was "My name is so-and-so and I'm an artist."

When I went to this meeting I did not for a moment think I had any problem with writing. It was probably the first time in my life that I did not think I had problems with writing. I had usually seen writing as hard – whether I was blocked or whether the writing was flowing. But that did not matter now, for I had in the past year quit writing. I was in art school – actually taking classes at many New York City art schools, and having the time of my life drawing and painting and working with clay. I didn't think I'd ever go back to working with words. I said as much, when it came my time to speak.

The response was kind of unpleasant. No one had a word to say about this happy development in my life, my discovery that I could draw and paint and even sculpt. I was actually having some early success, and I mentioned it. Before this I had never been a visual artist, but I was learning fast and in less than a year I had, twice in a row, had realistic paintings of women on exhibit at the Art Students League and up in the Catskills my painting of a blue tree was reproduced in the catalog of the Woodstock School of Art.

Still, the pleasure I was taking in visual arts made no impression on the Arts Anonymous people. What did seem to interest them was this awful problem they presumed I was having. No matter that I was getting great joy out of painting. They could not see why I would not be writing unless I was suffering from Writers' Block. "How sad," said an earnest girl in overalls. "How awful for you," said a middle-aged man wearing a T-shirt with Proust's picture on it. "I'll pray for you," said another earnest girl, who then brought out a small tape recorder and played for us a song about hope sung by Pat Boone's daughter. Most of the talk that evening came from writers, none from composers, and there were only a couple of visual people, both of them joyless, both saying they needed discipline, both eager for commercial success, one as a portrait painter, the other as an illustrator, activities that clearly had little appeal to either of them. They were suffering, but the writers seemed to suffer the most. The writers who said they could not write. Either that or they were writing a little bit and it was a painful ordeal and it wasn't good enough.

The most vocal was a man with long hair and wild eyes, Harry, who said he had been a rock 'n roll journalist. Recently, he had had a great breakthrough in his career. He had signed a contract and taken advance money for a book, his first book, which was to be a history of disco music.

The idea had come from a publisher and Harry had leapt at the offer – even though he hated all disco music. His feelings about disco were beside the point, he said, because the important thing was that until now he had never had a book published. And now he was in real trouble because the deadline was nearing and he had not written a word about disco. And that was why, he said, he had come to this place looking for help.

The reason he could not write a word, he repeated, was that he hated his subject. But he kept insisting he had to write the book. Some of the people at the meeting backed him up, saying writing was always an ordeal and all he needed was greater discipline. Others suggested he try to get the publisher to agree to another subject, which he said would be impossible, and anyway hatred of disco should not stop what he called "a real writer" from writing its history. I suggested he simply drop the project – something that everyone who writes knows is frequently done. That too, he said, was absolutely impossible. He stressed that it was not the money that kept him from giving up, it was that it was so important to have a published book.

"All my life," he said, "I've wanted to be a writer." It did not matter that the book he wanted to do had nothing to do with his own life, nothing to do with any music he cared about. He wanted to be a published writer.

It was a little like something I had encountered a few years back in Washington when working on a magazine article about the shockingly small handful of U.S. Foreign Service Officers who resigned in protest over American war criminal acts in Vietnam, Cambodia and Laos. One of them, Tony Lake, a well-presented boyish man who put his interviewer at ease, would later become National Security Adviser but for the moment was in exile at a private museum featuring antique decorative arts. He seemed like one of those people destined to be successful at something very respectable, like becoming a controlling executive in public broadcasting, or president of a liberal arts college. Instead, he had risen to a post on the National Security Council under Henry Kissinger. He said that only after he resigned did he realize why he had stayed so long even though hating the work and hating the direction in which American foreign policy was moving – stayed on even while hundreds of thousands of civilians were being mutilated and killed in Southeast Asia because of stupid, vindictive things he and the others who ranked high in America's foreign policy system were doing.

The reason he had stayed on so long in the Foreign Service, he said, was of course that he really believed he could move policy in a decent direction, but there was also the factor that he liked the picture he had of himself as one day being a distinguished, retired ambassador.

It sounded to me that Tony Lake had been in the same sort of situation as that of a person who wanted to be A Writer.

A retired ambassador. A published writer. Not a person. Not something important unfolding. Just a title.

writer at play

I had listened carefully to that young man who was serious about his music, had been commissioned with an advance to write a book about disco music (which he detested) and was seeking help because mysteriously he was not able to write a word. I knew then what the trouble was. It was simply that there was nothing connected to who he was in what he was attempting to write.

I knew that because I realized that all too often what I had been writing and getting published had little meaning for me. And now it was a time when many things in my life were changing and I was finding writing of little help. And then, not quite getting the message, I was thrown into despair because I just could not finish the writing that I was so certain I wanted to accomplish.

It had seemed like a particularly good time in my long career as a professional writer. A journalist friend, Max Vanzi, and I had this new book in the stores about the Philippines and its rapacious martial law leaders and its underground revolutionary opposition – the book a first-hand exposé which, now that it was published, was getting attention. Some people liked it. Foreign policy establishment people hated it. When a new book is getting attention from those who hate it as much as from those who like it, it is an ideal time to get new book contracts.

I had not focused yet on how long it had been since I had written anything without a contract. But I had these plans, and it seemed like really a perfect time. I had a new apartment, small but with south light, looking down on a garden and out over miles of rooftops from West 25th Street. And I was just free of a slow-dying marriage. And I had ideas – a proposal for a book exposing with great irony bizarre but entertaining sex and personal development things in California, things that in life but not writing I might actually like. Or a book about the five greatest rivers of the world. Or a travel series based on the lie that all through the Bahamas and the West Indies there are magnificent vestiges of spectacular old mansions and forts and monuments from some grand colonial era, rather than sorry vestiges of a depressing and brutal and greed-filled slave labor time. Not an unusual lie in the world of travel writing, but a lie nonetheless.

The first of my book plans to find a home was this one based on the outright lie. Some months later I returned from the Bahamas, and from a very blonde photographer who had gone there with me. It had gone badly with the woman, and all those beaches and hotels filled me with boredom verging on loathing. I was in a depression so deep that at first I did not think of it as depression, but rather as an objective and mysterious set-back. I continued to send out my proposals.

The one consolation when I did that final travel writing project more than 25 years ago was that there are even worse things that people do and call themselves writers. Most business "writing" falls in this category, for reimbursement goes well beyond the free accommodations given to travel writers in exchange for lying. In most, if not all, business writing you are being paid directly or indirectly to lie to promote clients who do harm.

(But travel writing is the silliest. When very young and down and out I lived for a time in a costly suite in Hong Kong's fanciest hotel, the Peninsular, sneaking in fish and chips – there was still bad but cheap English food around – because the free-loading deal did not include food. A guy I knew then in Bangkok, who was as broke as me, had so many free plane tickets that when he got really hungry he would fly to Singapore and back or to Saigon and back or to Manila and back for the sake of the airline meals.)

The next step down from travel writing is ghost-writing – which is a way out for people scared to death of their own stories.

And one step below reducing yourself to another person's ghost is the pretentious falsification of what is real in the name of fiction.

At the very bottom is falsification of your own story.)

The big plan in this blocked time that now seemed on the way to a publishing deal was for this book that had been a fellow writer's idea about what he considered my amusing family. It would be about my late and distinguished Victorian-style grandfather who had been an internationalist early in the century and had won a Pulitzer prize for fiction. It would be about my years of travel and adventure and sometimes even involvement in left-wing revolution. And also about my twin brother, the proper twin, who roamed the world almost as much as I did but not for the same reasons, since he was on the other side – doing his traveling for usually secret government agencies, most recently the CIA.

A light family-experience book, much like the books that my father once published with considerable success. The writer friend said it should probably be titled *Twins in the American Century*. (This seemed plausible, in the mid-eighties, which no one except Gore Vidal seemed to know was the last point at which there would be non-ironic talk of "the American century." I wrote a proposal. An editor at MacMillan said a contract would be drawn up as soon as I could produce a sample chapter.

I couldn't write a word. Writers' block had never been this bad.

In desperation I looked in the library on 23rd Street for help, and found a book published by Writers' Digest Press (which I had always considered a con operation) called something like *The Natural Way to*

Overcoming Writers' Block. It was by a woman who put forth the thesis that each writer has deep inside him or her a little boy or a little girl who wants to come out and play. Giving your little boy or girl permission to play was what would end writers' block.

I had not thought till I read this book that my depression could get even worse.

And then there came from somewhere inside me an embarrassing uproar. Here I was well along in what I looked upon as a serious if checkered career of writing and adventure, and here I was, just turned 50, having never written a word about the first 18 years of my life. And now sadness was chasing out anger was chasing out sadness was chasing out anger was chasing out crying was chasing out fury and sadness and anger – with this surprising lost child coming from some lost place just as if he were and always had been real – and the last thing he wanted to do now that he was back was come out and play. He wanted to rage. He wanted revenge, and he did not care just now how many dead and injured would be left in his wake.

the forgiveness question

That night we were cheering for patricide.

A pretty girl with blue eyes stood up with that day's *New York Post*, held it high in front of her so that all 30 or so people in the room could see the front page, on which there was a picture of a younger pretty girl, this one billed as a Long Island cheerleader, who had proudly admitted that she had just shot her father, who had been molesting her for years. Everyone in the room applauded.

For this group, the first organization I ever joined voluntarily, was made up of people on the hunt for what had happened in the often far distant past, this 12-step organization called Adult Children of Alcoholics, ACOA, which in Manhattan violated all 12-step rules, showed no respect for praying nor for confession that was not geared to going after the villains.

In a typical meeting, everyone would join hands at the end. But I remember a time when instead of closing with the Serenity Prayer or the Our Father, as in orthodox 12-step meetings, the person leading the meeting said firmly, "Fuck forgiveness," and everyone seemed ready to go forth joyfully into the world.

In Manhattan there were these meetings all over town, a meeting somewhere at almost any time of night or day. When it got near Christmas or Mother's Day you could hear the shouts a block away. But support was the point. Support in hearing stories the teller had known for years but had not found a place to bring them.

Often the people who came, often people long traumatized, had been in therapy for many years without ever being invited to focus in any but the most superficial ways on what had happened in their most formative years. Often they had joined groups supposedly dedicated to giving support but the support was to be told to banish anger, be forgiving, live by affirmations.

False change was never promoted here in ACOA. There might be some recognition that people of the past did all they could, but that did not let the villains off the hook. Change that was honored here involved turning the tables on family people of the past whose versions of stories had been meant to silence abused children. And it was profoundly freeing, I found, to have this kind of support for things that were supposed to be unspoken – family alcoholism being the least of it in these free-flowing meetings.

The 12-step movement overall, in all its branches, is profoundly subversive in that people, if usually not so vociferous as in ACOA, tell and retell their own stories without a therapist or social worker or clergy member present to set the limits. It is the bane of second-rate therapists and other slow, would-be authorities. Sometimes, however, it seemed to me that real change was not very welcome even in the free-wheeling context of ACOA.

I noticed that although when a person entered the program it could become that person's entire life, few stayed much more than a year. And in retrospect I suspected this was because the new stories become as frozen in place as the old stories. Not that I advocated constant forgiveness. But there was this matter of the nature of purely spoken stories: for it is in the nature of stories told verbally that they are not likely to live and grow and change. They can be bolstered, but they of necessity must move towards predetermined endings – it being almost impossible to tell a story out loud without knowing where it will go.

Still, it was a huge thing to be around people who had gotten into previously forbidden territory. It was wildly liberating to finally bring one's own story to speech. At first I felt alienated by expressions of anger, and then I felt right at home, and came to savor the anger that was in the air. I would feel happy and light when someone I had come to know who combined anger with clarity entered one of the meeting rooms – such as a woman whose father was a cult psychiatrist, or an artist who had been pigeon-holed as a lawyer. And I would bellow complaints of my own from a tight dark early life that I had suppressed.

And there was one place in the program where stories were not cut off with predetermined endings. This place, which seemed so conducive to change and growth, was a late Sunday morning meeting held on the stage of a small theater inside St. Vincent's Hospital in Greenwich Village. I would walk down there from Chelsea. It was billed as a fourth-step meeting, the fourth-step in regular 12-step meetings being that point at which you write out the important things of your life to discover, among much else, to whom you must "make amends." These Manhattan meetings horrified visitors from much gentler ACOA and other 12-step programs in other boroughs and other towns. No one in Manhattan ACOA was much interested in making amends if that got in the way of truth.

It might seem that after many meetings a person's stories were set in place forever. But in this supposed fourth-step meeting on the stage at St. Vincent's there were no spoken stories. All these stories were written. At first I missed the bombast – the shouting and crying and roaring – of the other meetings. Then I found that far more was happening here than in any of the other meeting rooms.

The format was that someone would put a series of questions on a blackboard, and everyone would write out answers, and later read aloud what they had written.

It was in here that when answering a question about birthdays I discovered I could remember nothing of birthdays, which being a twin were always, this part I remembered, played up way in advance. But now the camera in my mind could find only blankness, except for one scene where my parents throw us a birthday party at a beach place, and I was at a baseball diamond there, and once again I was the last one to be picked by the captains, my brother one of them, who did the choosing. And from that scene so much unfolded that had been locked away as if banished forever from memory. So much that made life possible.

And it was here at the St. Vincent's meeting that I put together my own stories by putting together what I had experienced in the stories of my close relatives – as in the story of my Cousin Margaret, who recently had said she wanted to die of apparently curable cancer and did die. And the vibrant cousin-by-marriage who had just hung herself in Rochester while her husband was with his girlfriend, and they said in her family and mine how lucky the husband was for he now could get on with his life. And my favorite cousin who was now in a battered women's shelter and who, it had just come out, had been fucked and beaten nearly every day by her brother from the time she was too small to be entered until his strange death on the road when she was sixteen.

It was in writing that I finally shed the family story that this mostly accomplished family might be humorless but was no worse than comic in a pretentious Victorian way. I wrote and as I wrote memory returned.

So far I did not really think of myself as writing in this time. I still thought of myself as living purely in visual worlds.

But it surely was writing – and then expanding the writing by reading it out loud to others – the ancient and profound version of publishing. Just as something changes when a story goes from the head to the paper, so too something happens when the written story is brought to speech.

For while reading aloud a written piece the writer is often more surprised by what happens than is the listener – as was the case when I read what I wrote about twins sharing a birthday. Previously unhonored parts of a story cause surprising reactions in the writer as much as in the listener. Reading about birthdays, I had to pause and go slow because tears were coming. I did not know the depth or importance of the story until the reading was underway.

These St. Vincent's meetings were much on my mind as Authentic Writing began. But I did not forget the other meetings. In my last months in ACOA I did keep going to the non-writing meetings too, if only to join in the chorus of "fuck forgiveness."

"Fuck forgiveness" was not quite so clear-cut as "fuck the begrudgers." But this motto too is useful to writers who are on the way to what is most real and do not want to stop before they get to the story. Writers who are on the way, and who may want to forgive, but can be stopped by premature forgiveness.

in a darkened theater

Sitting in darkness in Manhattan's Kraine Theater – surrounded by music – in the glow of the stage – music from instruments and voices and the pure music of words – and movement with words as performed – even into dance – and all of it framed in a complex system of visual richness – it took the sound and lighting man many hours to set up the bare stage – and it was now so in order that you never thought it was part of a carefully worked-out scheme – the combination of spontaneity and rehearsal – words and music – song and light.

Here on this January night of an Authentic Writing *Song and Story* performance I thought of the deep contempt I had had 40 years back when I lived with expatriates in the Anafiotika district of Athens – which seemed to me the sort of perfect bohemian setting – laughter and retsina and tightly abandoned tavern dancing – as far removed as you could be from things like the family I came from and the silly order of gray Eisenhower America – there in one of these very small white-washed houses perched on the side of the Acropolis – you could look up from the roof and see the Parthenon – and down on the roofs of other foreigner's houses – and with a view out and over, it seemed, not just Athens but all of Attica, all of the world. Still unamplified bouzouki music by taverna tables set on the steps in the winding lanes, between the white-washed sides of these houses – lanes where what might be pebbles beneath your feet were as likely to be fragments of ancient pottery or Byzantine mosaic.

Here with a lovely girl, Vannie – who painted all day and never wrote – while I, who slept much of the day, never painted but wrote hour after hour all through almost all of the nights.

And we both had such contempt for Dawn from London who could not decide whether she wanted to be a painter or a writer and did neither – or Harold from Hot Springs, Arkansas who had in progress a series of paintings of floating handkerchiefs and wrote poetry that he was proud no one could untangle – or pretty Mary from Dublin who modeled and wanted to act – or Daniel from Chicago who was about ready to give up this life so as to pursue a doctorate in English, or Jason from Queensland, who bragged of his days off the coast of Somalia as, he said, the last of the white dhow skippers – and was now, he said, outlining a poem – to be his first – an epic poem – and thinking too, it seemed, of taking up etching – or Harold Winterbotham from Dorset who knew what he was doing, he said, because every winter he went home and spent three months with his mother in an English village where he came into himself because he always wrote and produced and starred in the village church's annual play whereas in Anafiotika he was also an abstract painter – or dim-witted Klaus from Frankfurt who went to Nasser's Egypt and heard things about Jews that made him think his S.S. father might have been right, and now he painted fuzzily – and played a lute.

Such contempt I had, and maybe Vannie did too, for anyone who did not have a serious course and did not follow through – for anyone who could not be one thing or another – could not keep it separate.

A view that I held until my life depended on light and shade and form and line and color – and at another time on sound and movement and song – my life and my writing too.

All whirling around in my mind in this time in the dark in the Kraine Theater where I was suddenly thinking of a time in the deceptively clear light of Greece when I feared mere dilettantism if I could not be simply and solely one thing or another.

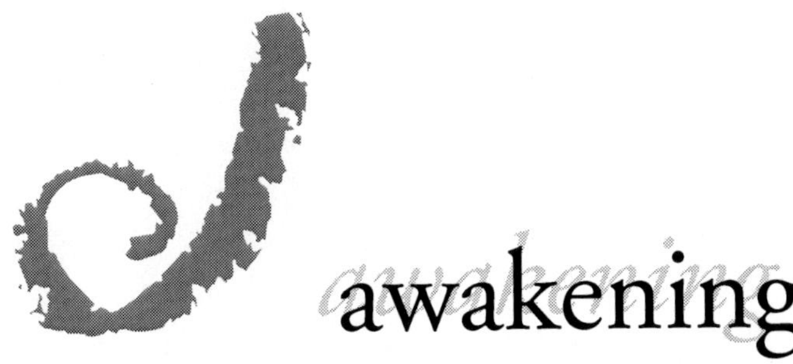

awakening

One night I dreamt that I was on a stage, a theater, an actual Fourth Street theater, either the Red Room or the Kraine, a stage that was familiar but also new to me, as it is in life, new and familiar, these places where Suzanne Bachner based her theater company, and where in collaboration with her company we were staging Authentic Writing performance events. Where it was proving true that a certain kind of theater person was our natural ally – actors who, like the kind of writers we support, know that to practice their art and craft they must go deep inside.

In the dream I am at first talking with Suzanne, something to do with something I could do in connection with whatever they are doing. Something I could create and put on here. Then she leaves me alone. Leaves me alone so I can come up with ideas, or maybe leaves me alone because she has no faith I will have ideas but is willing to indulge me in my desire to use the space. So now I am alone in the dark on the stage. There are lights in the theater, for work is in progress there, cleaning work and renovation work, but the curtain is down and so I can just barely see where I am. Then suddenly the stage lights come on and I am before an audience. And there is music coming up, music in my head that accompanies me as I stride about, make sweeping gestures – but for what? I have no idea what – though I know there is something in the same way that sometimes when I sit down to write I have no idea of what to write but faith that there is something of substance waiting.

Someone knocks on a post beside the curtain to see if anyone is here, then pulls the curtain back and steps in. It is one of the people working in the theater. He is surprised anyone is here. But he does not seem at all surprised to see I have undressed and am wrapped in a sheet, like a toga. He says excuse me, picks up a small table, and leaves. Clearly, to him everything here is quite normal.

I am striding about again, in my normal clothes now, looking in different directions, making gestures, hearing the music, and although it is still silent here I am singing away in my head to the music that is in my head, words and music while I move about the stage, pushing something ahead, though I do not know yet what it is.

I am alone after I leave the theater. This does not surprise me since in dreams I am almost always alone. For a moment I am speaking with my friend Eileen whom I sometimes, in this dream version, meet for dinner in the city before I return to Woodstock just as I did a couple of times years ago in waking life. She tells me now that she can't meet me this way any longer before my 100-mile trip because Manhattan is a 20-minute subway ride away from her place in Brooklyn and so she would get home too late.

I wake up in Woodstock, excited about this show I am about to do. I am unconcerned about Eileen. I have been in a nether world between sleeping and waking. I know the theater as a real theater, just as I know it when I am awake. I know I live in Woodstock and I will continue to come back here. I know I have worked with Suzanne and will work with her again. Know this when awake as well as when dreaming. I have had dinner in the city in the past with Eileen. It is usual for me to travel 100 miles at night from the city to Woodstock, where I am happy to live. None of this is merely a dream. But the lack of anyone else in my life is pure dream world.

And now I wake up and this thing I am trying to get to as I stride about the stage, moving to interior music, singing and ready to speak the lines I know will come for this thing I do not know except that I know it is there – this thing I knew in the dream was there is suddenly coming into focus. I am awake enough to know I am now in our bed but enough still in what may or may not be a nether world to also know the darkened stage I have just been on. And what is coming is no longer only a mystery, as it was while I was striding about that dark stage. So I get up, trying not to wake Marta, and start to write.

a song in my heart

I did not know that music was that important to me until I took my search for what had happened in light times and shadow times into the written word. And there I found that I, who did not sing, coming from a family where there was no singing, I who did not play musical instruments – had not even tried since childhood days with mail-order ocarinas and harmonicas and ukuleles plus an old, bent-neck guitar whose steel strings chewed up my fingers – I, who was not musical, was suddenly, many years later, as I wrote, finding music in almost every story. To such an extent that I realized I had long ago memorized the old songs that now kept appearing in those stories from early days. I still knew all the words and I still knew the tunes as well as I knew the words, even though I had not ever been considered musical.

The words, which was one thing since I thought myself fairly skilled with words. But the tunes too. And I found myself after half a century of never singing – not counting certain drunken episodes that had stopped 30 years back – found myself singing with so little humility that I began doing song-and-story stage performances. Actually singing now, 50 years after a glee club director in boarding school told me I could not sing, said it to me the way English teachers (though thank God not mine back then) tell boys and girls they have no "talent" for writing.

And anyway I had no choice now – for to run from the songs now would be the same thing as running from the story – which is what happens if the context is left out – here a crucial part of the context of the scenes of my stories so often being music. To neglect the music now would be the coward's way out. So I took voice lessons and even studied music theory.

Crucial parts of the context of stories going back to the secret life I led in childhood, where my upstairs yellow room was in the back of an old Connecticut house. And my room had a wobbly old second-story outside staircase, by which I could sneak out and away from family – away from how I was told life was supposed to be. This world of mine in this back room, with a radio hidden under the covers, my life made rich by what came from Wheeling, West Virginia late at night where I found myself down on the levee, the levee so low, late in the evening I hear the wind blow. And wonderful nonsense words and sounds – mairzy doats and dozy doats, and chickery chick cha-la,cha-la. And those Irish radio songs that no one in this Anglophile family would know or admit to knowing – swinging with my sister Kate on a garden gate, seeing the sun go down on Galway Bay, and old Kilarney and Glocca Morra – was there really such a place? Did it matter when Irish eyes are smiling? A world that was not the world I was supposed to stay in.

Without the songs there were empty places in the story, blank places where there should be context, not blankness. As I wrote so many years later, it was becoming increasingly clear that stories would be empty stories if I ruled out that part of the context. The songs.

Early on a pitch-black freezing morning in boarding school there would be Frankie Laine, coming from a Boston radio station, telling how that lucky old sun has got nothing to do but roll around heaven all day. Or the new songs from Broadway – the corn is as high as an elephant's eye and there is nothing like a dame and some enchanted evening. And Doris Day, who had become a surprisingly sensuous night club big band singer in the movie *Young Man with a Horn*, and now this sexy voice coming out of radios: with a song in my heart I behold your adorable face, just a song at the start....

A song in my heart, coming into the dorm room and also playing at our sister school's dance where I learned partially skin-on-skin necking – and in the summers in the White Mountains when we fixed up the intentionally rustic old Playhouse, which had been used for charity dances in an exalted past before we were born, and now we made the Playhouse our own, lights so low we danced in darkness to this song – all the kids and me and Kitty, my true love, to whom I wished I could sing about how I always knew I would live life through with a song in my heart for YOUUUUUUU.

This context. I'm just a poor wayfaring stranger. It's almost like being in love. I have too much of Texas in my heart. It might as well be spring. These vital sources of hope and information.

real writing means war

All writers should be warned that real writing – writing that goes beyond predictable matters, or pure genre hokum, or fluffy, teddy bear stories – real writing invariably means war.

It is almost never good news to a family that a family member is writing. It is terrible news that someone may go public with, among other things, his or her version of events in the family cult in which he or she once lived.

It is not just the possibility that family members might be portrayed as less than heroic characters – it is also that the entire surface world as they know it – everything seen as good and moral and everything that could be seen as deserving protection and all their careful sorting out the sheep from the goats – might turn out to be nothing more than clever theater designed to solidify and enhance and enforce whatever the position of the family's most triumphal members.

When I was 36 and I got a contract and advance money from a major publisher to complete a novel, my brother and a cousin I respected let it be known I was behaving in really bad taste because I was celebrating the contract with Dom Pérignon and Beluga caviar. Our family had not had a writer since my grandfather, who won the Pulitzer

Prize for fiction in 1917, and I – more innocent than I was ready to admit – thought that my success would please them.

But it was just the opposite. The family already had had its writer. It was presumptuous for anyone else to try.

I wrote off my twin's reaction to jealousy, he being the good twin who was expected to be rewarded for being good. I found it sad and touching that he was telling people I should not have gotten such a contract because I had done all the wrong things in life, most notably never having had the benefit of graduate school.

My father's reaction was just as negative, even though he was a publisher, or maybe because he was a publisher. And even though he was the only one in the family who had seemed sympathetic to my writing. I had gotten this contract without him and his contacts, but in past years, right back to college, he had been helpful to the point of linking me up with agents and editors. But now he took me to lunch at the staid old Century Club to tell me I had become the family's number-one problem since I did not have a proper job. I had thought the lunch was to celebrate my triumph. And as for a job, I had my book advance.

"Your grandfather never took a cent until a book was in print," my father said. As a writer I had been around writers and publishing people for years and I had never heard of any other case of a writer refusing a book advance until after the book was done. Maybe it was because my grandfather, unlike me and most writers, had an independent income. But I don't really think that explains it – so here is yet something more about this strange family to explore.

This opposition to writing from my family was especially blunt and blatant – but in kinder, gentler families than mine it is also common that the opposition is there. Whether it comes in the form of "Please write something inspirational" or "If that's what you want to do you'd better get your real estate license."

Recently I made the mistake of showing my brother what I had written about that time during the war when we were nine and they forgot about us in Florida, and although he stayed at the beach hotel and got credit for looking at fourth grade textbooks, I became a long-haired scraggly swamp rat, roaming the jungles and finding ways to get coins to play the slot machines at Max's tavern, where I was a regular. I thought that what I wrote and showed him portrayed his position as much more difficult than mine, he being called upon to be the perfect child while I was, in comparison, free to run, as only a family scapegoat can be.

I showed the story to my brother – about the mildest story I had ever written in which he appeared – I showed it even though I knew better.

"I can see that writing memoir is a real struggle for you," he said. "And I resent your writing this Florida story this way."

There was another way I could and should have written it, he said. I should have written that he too played the slot machines at Max's and roamed the jungles and got into rotten citrus fruit fights with local urchins. That he was more than just the trapped good little boy I had portrayed. And he repeated, "A real struggle for you."

And he sent me a letter, now not in anger, saying that in any case memoir is not the proper course. The problem with memoir, he said, is that you cannot resolve people's stories if you stick only to what actually happened. In memoir there are no proper endings.

I had showed him my story even though I knew enough by now never to show anything I wrote to a relative. I had seen it happen over and over – the reaction that nearly always means trouble. Sometimes it comes as something said sweetly such as "You should be commended for trying even if it proves to be too much for you." Sometimes the reaction is fierce, as in "How can you say such things about me or your mother (or father or brother or sister or grandparents or country or your Scout leader)?" Just the way critics were upset that the McCourt brothers did not depict their mother as if she were a mummified saint.

I have seen people from our workshops yanked away to another part of the country to keep them from writing. Or maybe, out of the blue, it is time to have another child, or maybe this is the moment to turn your life over to caring for dying relatives, which is what my brother once said I should do, or time to take a course in something decent like children's literature or technical writing – anything except writing about your life.

demons

The first few times I went into the story, I thought I had captured that strange time when I should have been on top of the world because my novel, an actual novel, was coming out, and did come out, published at the start of the seventies by a hot new house, Harper's Magazine Press, which was half owned by the ridiculously venerable and orthodox Harper & Row, the other half owned by *Harper's Magazine*, which was in turn owned by humorless Midwest newspaper tycoons and which also had been around since the beginning of time. But for just this moment *Harper's* was between its old stuffy version and a stuffier new version, and for this moment it was the hottest magazine in town. It was run by Willie Morris, a young, celebrated Southern writer who was riding the crest and had recently become the most exciting and cool and irreverent magazine editor in New York City. He drove the nervous owners of the two Harpers crazy. His magazine caused talk all over town and way beyond, which to the owners was not a gentlemanly thing to do. Among those who could appear in the office any day might be Norman Mailer or some other famous writer, or some angry feminist, or somebody from the suddenly surging gay rights movement, or someone advocating bomb throwing – all the things most editors, as over at the *New York Times*, were sweeping under the rug.

Harper's Magazine Press, run by another exciting editor named Herman Golub, was in with Willie's magazine, not with staid old Harper & Row. The magazine office, in a Park Avenue South building with two bars down below, was where I spent so many of my days now. It was filled with boisterous, often drunk and famous people, and some famous ones who stopped with a couple of beers, such as Bill Moyers, who, like me, was on the small spring list, but did not drink the way I and some of the others did.

All these new and exciting friends to drink with. Which got me to front tables at Elaine's and parties where a middle-of-the-road celebrity might be Sargent Shriver or David Rockefeller. And there in the stores now was my mostly true-story novel, filled with eroticism and violence in Bangkok, a story that was up-to-the-minute topical since American soldiers were still at the time of publication getting five-day leaves to get laid in Bangkok, and spies of many nations were still racing around that sybaritic city, conning and assassinating each other. My name, which before I was ever published I'd made into a pretentious three-name author's name, was nearly as large as the title, *Where Dragons Dwell*. On the back was me in a hungover Humphrey Bogart pose with a cigarette dangling from the corner of my mouth. And in this time, first getting the book accepted, then spending the advance as I moved about the world wrapping up chapters, and then the pre-publication months with all the parties that I was now entitled to, and finally the aftermath with the book in a few bookstore windows – all this just in time, for I was 36. And in truth this time was in so many ways one of the worst times in my life – the deep feelings of hopelessness, the crazed drinking, a new doomed affair with a publishing girl. And if alone after the drinking, middle-of-the-night international phone calls to ex-girlfriends and girls I thought might have been girlfriends. Anyone who might love me. So bad I moved in mid-winter to a waterside cottage that had no phone. Ever deepening depression. Remorse. Near fatal loneliness.

Then the end. Two months after publication, the book still out there, it was the week I was supposed to be addressing the formidable Middlebury Writers Conference, where I had hoped for groupies, or at least praise. Instead I went to the airport and flew to Beirut, which once in the past, when I was on my way to Africa, I had found to be a profoundly discouraging city that rode on anti-Semitism and pretended to be like Paris. When I had been there before I had also found it so puritanical that my then girlfriend Vannie and I had had to claim we were cousins to get a hotel room together (incest was fine, but nothing else). This place, pre-civil-war Beirut, the end of the world. What had gotten into me?

When years later I wrote about that year, 1971, the year I was 36 and being published, the story kept changing. The first couple of times I stepped back into that time it seemed crystal clear that my destructive depression then had to do, on a direct line, with the family of origin. As clear as that C follows B follows A. For so many years I had tried hard not to think about those people who qualified as my nearest and dearest – my father, himself a publisher, sometimes generous but now telling me how bad it was that I had this novel, and how awful that I was living on advance money and did not have a regular job. My mother, the smartest one in the family, telling me, as she drank, and as my father told me, what a thorn I was in the family's collective side. And my old college roommate, who by now had married the widow of a publisher and moved into Upper East Side Waspdom, where he and his wife served popovers and floating island, was no more encouraging. And my twin brother was telling everyone who would listen that it was just plain wrong. So in my mind when I went back into the story there were, at first, no loose ends. In the version that came first, B followed A and C followed B, the villains were all in the family or close to it, and there were no more questions about the near suicidal despair that hit me just as everything was working out.

But I had to go into the story again and again, for I kept coming upon less easy-to-explain parts. This return to the story was more than 20 years later. The Authentic Writing Workshops were underway, and now I saw that what had happened to me was what I was seeing happen to so many accomplished writers. For whatever the specifics of the writers' life stories, there are always these demons who fly in from some dark, formidable place to tell the writers they are nothing. All of them, even writers who might have the support of a father and a brother and an old friend. Even writers who might be garnering Pulitzer Prizes and American Book Awards.

The demons who tell anyone who innovates to get with the program, respect the old accepted writers, respect the views of your teachers, and anyone who writes in the *New York Review of Books*, and anyone who belongs to the Modern Language Association, and especially anyone in your family, whether the family is literate or not. If someone likes your writing, the demons whisper do not trust that person. Even if that person is the person you most love and/or the literary figure you most respect. Do not trust them. Who cares about your version? Anyone who is honest with you would say you offer nothing but self-indulgence, whiney self-indulgence. Any success is a fluke.

When I went back into the story of that time with *Harper's*, the sad ending becomes more and more inevitable, and less easy to explain. My late father may have contributed, and maybe my brother and my mother and my old roommate did too – but when I went back into the story they were the least of it.

As I kept going back into the story – which is what a writer has to do – it was not just my father and brother and old roommate that made me want to kill myself just as my writing career took off. The demons hate the fact that stories with loose ends just hang there raising questions and bringing discomfort to the smug. Only really bad books sew everything up in neat if synthetic ways, but this is something the demons want badly. The demons understand that the only resolution, the only closure, that counts is that you must renounce what you have done. Burn your manuscripts or distort them beyond recognition. And try, you sorry little confessional twerp, to force into being writing that will disturb none of the nice people. None of your betters. Sew it up. Force closure. Final closure almost never happens in life, but the demons insist upon closure. For it is life, including life found in art, that they, with the help of human critics, are out to destroy.

To the demons life is cheap.

summation

Authentic Writing? The beginning? I go all the way back to my joy when I first discovered writing, which may have been the Oz books, and something that was inside myself was sparked. And then my discovery of intensely real writing – Wolfe and Fitzgerald and Hemingway and Farrell and Salinger too when I was still quite young, and their stories were sparking my own stories. And I also go back to that dark time when it was first clear that academics and reviewers I encountered were out to bury creative work in silly criticism. And even worse, my discovery of how friends and lovers can do the same.

I go then to my own important times, getting on to my own stories at last, finding it was not too late to get into what was in my own memory – sometimes matters of unbearable beauty, sometimes with razor's-edge danger. The stories and the context.

As in a house on the side of the Acropolis, another house across from the glittering temples and palaces of Bangkok, a balcony next to a Minaret in the Levant. That present right now, that will be a past, remembering what it was like with my true love, and our Authentic Writing program, here beneath the mountain in Woodstock. And the deep past in a formal house called White Pines in the grand but scruffy

White Mountains of New Hampshire. Especially New Hampshire.

At one point, when I had started Authentic Writing but needed cash badly, I was teaching a class at a state college. I sat at my desk at the head of the class and talked with a young man who had an infinite number of tattoos and piercings and lived with a boa constrictor – the kind of person who came to my classes after word got around that you could write what concerned you most and that whatever you did you would get an A. I heard this man say, just after I had said again that a person's stories are sacred – I heard him say, "I think you mean that memory is sacred."

I thought at first I would handle in weekend retreats the important process of getting at a person's most real stories. Harness these matters of stories and their context and a person's true identity. I had been a writer, then a painter, and then I had plunged into theology in attempts to reach these matters of identity. Writing, painting and theology now all at the same time. And next I was going to become a retreat leader.

I would call this program "Recovering Our Stories." I planned it out carefully with expert advice from theologians and other mentors who had long roamed in the retreat field. I would get at this matter of each person's identity that gets so buried in theory and commentary and the stories that are imposed by family and country and other cults. A critical part of how I would do this would be through the written word, for nothing in my own life had gotten me closer to my story than writing. Not even painting from my life.

The written word. Not just any writing but writing as art – writing that involves the recreation of concrete reality – writing that can take surprising directions of its own for it entails entering the story, which means stepping into mystery (which is as good a description of art as it is of a spiritual life).

And then it dawned on me that what I would be doing would not be just a series of liberal retreats. And it would not be about all the many ways of getting at the story. It would be about what I now knew to be the most dangerous and most promising of all the ways to get at the story – the recreation of the story on the page. Doing it not as a purely linear process. Doing it as art. Writing the story without any previous commitment to how it would come out.

It would be about exploration and discovery – and so in the end it would be about the finest of fine writing. I was leery of writing workshops, which seem more about taming stories than about finding them. Most teaching of writing is about keeping it under control so that nothing disturbing happens. How awful to leave the teaching or facilitating of writing to critics and academics who are ready to put the lid on and keep it there.

I had to appeal to people committed to the art of writing from life. People committed to creation and recreation. Not mere journaling or theory-based therapy writing. Not writing about the story but getting into the story – for I had discovered at the start that once someone gets into the story, begins to recreate reality, the writing is automatically fine writing.

When I finally went all-out for my own alternative versions of reality – a continuing process – I moved along sometimes without writing. I had gotten close to the story by telling it verbally in sympathetic groups. There had been points where work with a counselor had helped. Certainly revisiting places and persons of the past had led to recovered memories. As did drawing and painting. And as I suspected would singing. All of these things help – but none had been so potent as the written word.

The first of my projected liberal retreats, scheduled for a Benedictine Monastery in Vermont, filled up. We were snowed out, and it was never rescheduled, because at this point things were moving so fast that a retreat not explicitly based on writing made no sense to me. "Recovering Our Stories" was superceded by Authentic Writing. The Authentic Writing Workshops.

Sometimes in literature there is a play within a play, as in *Hamlet*, or *Kiss Me Kate* or *A Chorus Line*, or memoirs that take in the making of this or that production – as in Bob Fosse's life, or Claire Bloom's, or Francis Ford Coppola's. Some people in the workshops have written stories in which there are key subsidiary stories about studying with

Stella Adler or Martha Graham. Some write stories in which the story inside the story, or surrounding it, is what is most important. In one notable case the destruction of the World Trade Center in the present frame the murder in the past by Klansmen of the author's father. And to some readers there is always a play within a play – an inner play, like an inner child, or something called the shadow side, or the capital "S" Subtext.

This book that is coming to an end is about the experience of writing – what helps, what hinders – and it is certainly better than those many books by people, many of them terrible writers, who glory in literary theory and give precise instructions about dramatic arc, and rhetorical modes and things like the Seven Rules of Narrative, and the need to wrap everything up so neatly that every story contains that closure that never exists in life. Wrap the stories up ever more tightly until the breath goes out of them.

There is a usually unbridgeable gap between the theory and the practice of writing – the gap between the art itself and the intellectualization of that art – a gap as big as that between a vibrant Hans Hoffman painting and a monograph by an art historian – or between a Beethoven sonata and a volume on music theory and appreciation – that gap between what is aroused by the works of Leo Tolstoy or Graham Greene or Frank McCourt and the prattling of deconstructionist critics.

And so within this book about writing there is the writer's story, the play within the play, the play that can surround the play. For if writing is an art on a level with other forms of art it must have life. And the only life a writer can really know with any certain thoroughness is the writer's own. And if the writer's work is not set in the context of the writer's life, there is nothing there to make certain it is a real account of reality.

I have written here about how my time in visual art – where line and form and color unfold in ways that always surprise the artist –

taught me about writing. And then how singing as raised in writing brought me even closer to my stories – which is something the carefully measured English professors in their ersatz Gothic lairs can never do.

I have told some of my own adventure stories and some of my own harder stories, and some of my coming-to-life stories. I have tried to depict some of the places of my past – bearing in mind Flannery O'Connor's dictum that writing that is not true to concrete reality, that falsifies reality, should be dismissed as pornography. And her further dictum that what is found in concrete reality is the only medium by which the spiritual can be approached.

Writing actual scenes that come from inside the writer is automatically a spiritual endeavor – for to do this entails stepping into places of mystery where I cannot know beforehand what I will find.

And this stepping into the story without wrapping it up prematurely is an echo of the theological idea that sin is that which is not authentic.

What I have done here is try to share scenes that to me gained importance when I wrote them but might have been forgotten or distorted if I had not written them, had dismissed or forgotten them – like an amnesiac wandering a battlefield with no memory of what the battle had been about.

I might have forgotten the most important scenes if I had stuck to stories worked out in an orderly way in my head and then told by speaking them rather than writing them. I might have forgotten them if I had not been able to get new pieces to the stories, and revised pieces, and new versions of endings that are constantly supplanting old endings – which happens on the page but rarely just in the head. I might have forgotten them if I did not, as I think all artists should, keep going back into the stories – going back in, over and over – usually finding something new and often crucial when I am there again. Computer programs are marketed that can show a would-be writer how to plot out a book or screenplay. But this is not writing, this soulless system, any more than it is writing to follow some frightened teacher's version of what in writing should or should not be allowed.

The scenes I must deal with over and again. Me a scraggly swamp rat, forgotten in my family, coming out of a Florida jungle to be photographed by passing tourists. Scenes that come in as uninvited surprises when I sit down to write.

The constantly recounted, set-piece family scene still there of that night before I was born when a lightning bolt came down a chimney and out a city-like fireplace at that formal mountain house called White Pines – and traveled 70 feet past silk and tassels, costly hardwood, a Steinway, a Nefertiti head, all the way to the far end of the formal main room and then went into another formal fireplace and up another chimney, into the cold raw night where there was no protection from the high and raw mountains that this house had seemed designed to nullify.

Back and forth over scenes, and the scenes always changing – if I wrote them. That perfect family place and perfect family becoming, when moving to the page, a place of evil inhabited by monsters – then another time becoming somehow more fine, if not so right as before – a place that could remain in the landscape of my life as the past unfolded from the present (as did the future unfold from the present). The perfect place becoming a wasteland, and then another time becoming populated, and then another time a place of first love, and then a place of awful danger again. And simultaneously my boarding school from long ago was changing too – because of writing – from being a nightmare place to a life-saving place – and back and forth. These changes. The complexities and necessity of reality.

And more scenes always come, and as I write I wait for something new to unfold from them. Turkish soldiers using a live cat as a football…a Javanese soldier way upriver in Kalimantan in a time of ritual cannibalism saying he'll take care of dinner, going out behind the tribal longhouse, putting three dum-dum bullets into the last chicken…in the lobby of the Merlin Hotel, filled with refugees from Kuala Lumpur's race riots, Western school girls singing "Please Mrs. Robinson" as a sickly new Prime Minister strides in waving a submachine gun while outside his Malays are shooting 10,000 Chinese…me walking through dark city streets in times of curfew, knowing that behind some of those black windows there are snipers…me lying one floor up from Irving Place in New York City, warm in summer, my arms around smooth, silky Anne Marie as through French doors come the 3 a.m. sounds of horses' hooves on cobblestone…or in a raw Taiwan winter with a lithe rural bathhouse-massage girl, the two of us fighting for the covers, like cranky middle aged married people in the suburbs….

An outdoor wedding that seems very much like a childhood dream way back in Connecticut – the dream of a wedding in which I am old enough to leave my noisy house of peril and start my life, this dream in which I am on an actual green hill that I can see from my actual childhood bed. I can see it through a screen door opening to the wobbly outdoor staircase that goes down and out towards the greenery – a private staircase because the room had been a unit of a rural Connecticut boarding house before the commuters snapped up all such places. This dream that broke up recurring dreams of poison rain and torturer-jailers – this dream that as a child had never seemed completely false, never seemed like one of those good-little-boy things that adults thought I would like – as in much later times adults thought I could like stories written with ironic detachment that helped the authors flee from the realities that frightened them.

And I have written about how when I left the cold practice of following outlines (which had gotten me published in the conventional way, which at best may on a few occasions have led to sex I might otherwise have missed), how when I left this cold and safe version of writing, there was no writing theory that could get me back to writing. For by now art, to me, was not clever plans, like those concocted by the octopus of the How-to-Write Industry or the bottom-feeding academics who rise to the surface to gobble up art. Art by this time in my life was a matter of life and death.

I had to find out what had happened – especially the complex story at the center of so much I had to tell – the story of my brother the good twin and me the bad twin, the two of us winding up, as if in extension of our childhood, on opposites sides in actual wars – each of us having to fight for a corner of life, though at other times surfacing as actual human beings with even hope, but then again coming back to the peril we were in. And it could have led to my death, maybe his too, when he was with certain U.S. agencies and I was sometimes underground with the opponents of America's favorite dictators – Somoza, Chiang, Suharto, Marcos. This good twin and bad twin situation that mirrored our long ago childhood.

If I could not get to this story and beyond it then I was not practicing art, and if there was no art, only logic, then my work and life would have narrowed down so far that nothing mattered. The much dreaded disease called Writers' Block would have been the least of it.

Writers' block. The friend of dictators who object to any versions of reality other than their own versions, which are fake and often effective, designed to impose on others the versions under which they themselves thrive. Thrive by taming art.

Dictators and their allies the demons who tell a writer that no one is interested in what you have to say, and anyway you say it badly. Every veteran writer knows the demons that say you cannot really write, you are a fraud, you should give up on your own versions and copy the versions of your betters.

Sometimes the demons win, and writers even destroy their written stories. But the demons do not always win.

For art keeps breaking out. Writing as art. This is my story. Demons but also art. This is the story of the Authentic Writing Workshops.

Let the demons be fucked.

Fred Poole spent the early adult decades of his life living by his wits as a writer and journalist, often on the edges of society in war zones around the world, wild nighttime cities and countries where the maps pictured no roads. During this time he published a number of books – none of which he would write the same way now – including the novel *Where Dragons Dwell* (McGraw Hill) and with Max Vanzi the exposé of the Marcos regime *Revolution in the Philippines* (Harper's Magazine Press).

When it became clear in mid-life that the travel and the professional writing were not leading anywhere except into predictability, Fred found himself drawn to art on canvas. It was here, in a land that had no words and no assumptions, only form and color, that he began to reach parts of himself that had long been buried.

After years immersed in oil paint, anatomy classes and museum visits followed by an equally deep immersion in progressive theology, Fred returned to writing. But now his writing was different. It was no longer dominated by a pre-determined product. It became unleashed as his painting had been unleashed, a movement not governed by logic and thought but by instinct and feel. His writing became an expression of his core beliefs about art and the crucial importance of a person's unique version of their own story, a version that has no loyalty to anyone except the person doing the writing.

Authentic Writing

The Movement

Since 1993 Fred Poole has been conducting the Authentic Writing program out of his home in Woodstock, New York, in Manhattan and in colleges and retreat sites across the Northeast United States. In 1998 he met the writer Marta Szabo who became not only his wife, but his close partner in love, life and art. Together they offer weekly groups (including one that is by phone so that people all over the country can participate) and longer retreats, and they often produce theatrical events that incorporate words, music and all art forms.

You can find out more at AuthenticWriting.com.